Excavating the Sutlers' House

Artifacts of
the British Armies
in Fort Edward
and Lake George

Excavating the Sutlers' House

David R. Starbuck

UNIVERSITY PRESS OF NEW ENGLAND
HANOVER AND LONDON

University Press of New England,
One Court Street, Lebanon, NH 03766
www.upne.com

Printed in China
5 4 3 2 1

Library of Congress Cataloging-in-Publication Data
Starbuck, David R.
Excavating the sutlers' house: artifacts of the British armies in Fort Edward and Lake George / David R. Starbuck
p. cm.
Includes bibliographical references.
ISBN 978-1-58465-818-4 (pbk.: alk. paper)
1. United States—History—French and Indian War, 1755–1763—Antiquities. 2. New York (State)—History—French and Indian War, 1755–1763—Antiquities. 3. Fort Edward (N.Y.)—Antiquities. 4. Lake George (N.Y.)—Antiquities. 5. Great Britain. Army—History—French and Indian War, 1755–1763. 6. Sutlers—New York (State)—Fort Edward—History—18th century. 7. Sutlers—New York (State)—Lake George—History—18th century. 8. Material culture—New York (State)—Fort Edward—History—18th century. 9. Material culture—New York (State)—Lake George—History—18th century. 10. Excavations (Archaeology)—New York (State)—Fort Edward Region. I. Title.
E199.S784 2010
973.2'6—dc22 2009026960

FRONTISPIECE. This selection of British artifacts from the Fort Edward sutling house was excavated between 2001 and 2008. From upper left and clockwise: delft ointment jars, wine bottle, tobacco pipe, delft bowl, Brown Bess bayonet, cufflinks, scabbard clip, buckle, bone knife handle, and Brown Bess butt plate.

Contents

Preface

For eighteen years my colleagues and I have been excavating British military sites in Fort Edward and Lake George, New York, the setting for the largest British forts and encampments of the French and Indian War. Some of these sites had witnessed prior excavations, but our projects represent the most determined effort to understand the lifestyles and material culture of the British soldiers and officers who fought in the colony of New York during the 1750s. Since 1991 we have conducted extensive excavations in both of these communities, and we have processed and identified the artifacts from several extremely significant British sites. We have published quite a few articles and books that serve as progress reports for our work, but until now no synthesis has appeared that presents an overview of the artifacts left behind by British armies at archeological sites in northern New York State.

There are many good reasons for preparing this book at this time, and perhaps the best is that in 1996 Matthew Rozell, a history teacher in the Hudson Falls High School and an experienced avocational archeologist, discovered the remains of a 1750s sutlers' (merchants') house on the east bank of the Hudson River in Fort Edward. This was one of the essential points of supply from which goods were sold to British armies throughout the late 1750s. After preliminary research, we realized that there is very little literature about sutling houses and that none of them had ever been professionally excavated. After completing our work at other sites, we began digging the sutling house in 2001, and over a span of eight years we have recovered a fascinating range of artifacts from its enormous, filled-in cellar hole. This has convinced me that it is time to focus attention on the rich and varied material culture brought to this region by British armies and their suppliers some two hundred and fifty years ago. The discoveries made at the sutlers' site in Fort Edward could stand alone very easily, but clearly it is preferable to also include representative artifacts found at the many points of consumption: the British forts and encampments throughout the region that received goods from the civilian sutlers who were attached to each camp.

That is why this volume has brought together some of the most distinctive British artifacts that we have excavated from: (1) the sutling house in Fort Edward, (2) Rogers Island in the Hudson River in Fort Edward, (3) the fort in Fort Edward, (4) Fort William Henry in Lake George (from excavations by Stanley Gifford in the 1950s and our own excavations in the 1990s), and (5) artifacts that we excavated from the Lake George Battlefield Park (Fort George) in 2000–2001. After eighteen years of research, it has become possible to present British artifacts that reflect forts and camps across a sizeable region and an entire war, and not just the finds from a single camp. This should greatly broaden this book's utility for reenactors, historical archeologists, and museum specialists.

I am indebted to Adirondack Community College in Queensbury, New York, for sponsoring archeological summer field schools for all of these years, and to Plymouth State University, part of the University System of New Hampshire, for allowing me the time each summer to research some of the most intact military sites in the northeastern United States. I also wish to thank the Rogers Island Visitors Center, the Fort Edward Historical Association, the Fort William Henry Corporation, the New York State Department of Environmental Conservation, and the Fruitful Vine Christian Church for allowing me access to collections owned or housed by each of them. Paul McCarty, Town and Village Historian for Fort Edward, and Eileen Hannay, Manager of the Rogers Island Visitors Center, were especially helpful.

Many individuals have assisted with the processing and preliminary identification of these artifacts, and I wish to acknowledge Elizabeth Hall, Merle Parsons, Maureen Kennedy, Matthew Rozell, John Farrell, June Talley, Pat Meaney, Brad Jarvis, Sarah Majot, Lyn Hohmann, and Amanda Allen. Elizabeth Hall, in particular, has spent an enormous amount of time processing and identifying artifacts from every one of these sites, and it was she who tabulated most of the artifacts from the sutlers' site.

Paula Dennis of In the Field Consulting has photo-edited and enhanced nearly all of the older photographs and maps that appear in this volume, taken over a period of many years. This has greatly helped the appearance of the images of many of the artifacts to which we no longer have access.

Phil Dunning of Parks Canada helped with the interpretation of the Fort Edward sutling house and its artifacts. His knowledge as a modern-day sutler helped refocus several of my interpretations, and it was Phil who persuaded me that our sutling house would also have served as a tavern.

Karlis Karklins, retired from Parks Canada, examined our glass beads and provided the bead identifications that appear in Chapter 9. Timothy J. Todish, Jerry Olson, Lynn Evans, and Daniel Sivilich all provided useful interpretations of other artifacts. Tim Todish has proven to be a wonderful, continuing source of information about all aspects of the French and Indian War.

Charles Vandrei, Agency Historic Preservation Officer for the New York State Department of Environmental Conservation, provided images of some of the artifacts excavated from the Lake George Battlefield Park.

Oliver Hoover, International Editor for the American Numismatic Society journal *Numismatic Literature*, provided much-appreciated assistance with some of the coin identifications, and it was Oliver who first informed me that we had discovered an Oak Tree Shilling in 2006 (not a Pine Tree Shilling, as we had previously supposed). Another important coin identification was provided by John Farrell, who identified the 1695 French liard found in the Fort Edward sutling house.

Phyllis Deutsch, editor-in-chief for the University Press of New England (UPNE), has been instrumental in bringing this book to completion, and Kathy Kimball at UPNE was responsible for the design for this volume. I am extremely grateful to both of them.

Finally, a word of explanation. At the suggestion of Merle Parsons, I have begun each chapter with a quotation from the diary of Jabez Fitch, Jr. (1968). Fitch served in Fort Edward in 1757 and 1758, and his diary is a wonderful source of insights into life on the British northern frontier during the French and Indian War. Fitch even made many references to the sutlers from whom he personally purchased supplies.

March 2009 D.R.S.

Excavating the Sutlers' House

FIG. 1.1. French and Indian War reenactors marching on Rogers Island, September 23, 2006.

"our Men were Extreem Resolute"
—Jabez Fitch, Jr.
(August 10, 1757)

I

The British Encampments in Fort Edward and Lake George

NORTHEASTERN NEW YORK State is home to some of the most significant eighteenth-century military sites in the United States, created during both the French and Indian War and the American Revolution. Beginning with the Battle of Lake George in September of 1755, and continuing intermittently until September of 1783, British, French, and Colonial armies, together with their Native American allies, waged war along the waterways of the region and left behind the remains of a great many forts, entrenchments, battlefields, blockhouses, encampments and cantonments, along with literally thousands of artifacts that help to tell the story of the men (and a few women) who found themselves caught up in the hardships of the frontier wars (Starbuck 1999b).

The struggles they endured continue to have meaning for modern audiences, and their stories are told at several major museums and historical sites, including Fort William Henry, Fort Ticonderoga, Crown Point State Historic Site, Saratoga National Historical Park, and the Lake George Battlefield Park, and also at many smaller attractions that include the Fort House Museum, the Wing–Northrup House, and the Rogers Island Visitors Center in Fort Edward, the Lake George Historical Association, the Clinton County Historical Museum, and elsewhere. Most of these institutions prominently display artifacts that were in use during the colonial wars and in the war for independence. Some of these materials have always been held within museums or family collections, while others were obtained through archeology or amateur collecting. It is always preferable to have exact proveniences for excavated materials because this allows for better interpretation, but no matter what the source, artifacts provide an excellent opportunity for the public to appreciate the things of the past. The pleasure that comes from seeing or holding a bayonet, a musket ball, or even a broken hinge is a very tangible and exciting way for visitors of the twenty-first century to connect with those who struggled to survive in our region in the eighteenth century. This is especially true for the many thousands of reenactors who recreate the lives and stories of eighteenth-century soldiers and strive to replicate their material culture as accurately as possible (fig. 1.1) (Starbuck 2008b).

Artifact Studies

This is a book about artifacts, and specifically those that have been excavated from British military sites in Fort Edward and Lake George, New York (fig. 1.2). Most of these artifacts are from sites of the French and Indian War (1754–1763), but many of these sites were reoccupied during the Revolution, so there undoubtedly is some admixture of materials from the later war. It is appropriate to include artifacts from both Lake George and Fort Edward in this volume because the same armies and the same leaders occupied these two communities, and during the same handful of years they traveled back and forth on the Old Military Road that connected the two forts. Also, the same historical sources and maps typically cover both forts, and the material culture is the same. The many archeological digs conducted in these two towns have provided much useful contextual information for the artifacts, as well as insights into what was important to eighteenth-century British soldiers and officers.

Archeologists, historians, and reenactors all have a need for accurate identification guides, and archeologists in particular need to compare their findings with those from other archeological sites in order to understand regional and chronological differences in consumption patterns. Some of the guides commonly used by those who specialize in military sites are helpful to *all* historical archeologists, e.g., *A Guide to Artifacts of Colonial America* by Ivor Noel Hume (1970), and *Studies in Material Culture Research*, edited by Karlis Karklins (2000). There also are military site reports that have exceptionally thorough artifact descriptions, notably *Fort Michilimackinac 1715–1781* by Lyle Stone (1974); *Casements and Cannonballs* by Lee Hanson and Dick Ping Hsu (1975); and *Archaeological Investigation of Fort Ligonier 1960–1965* by Jacob L. Grimm (1970). Just as important are the non-archeological books that are collections-based, such as *Collector's Illustrated Encyclopedia of the American Revolution* by George C. Neumann and Frank J. Kravic (1975); *Colonial Wrought Iron: The Sorber Collection* by Don Plummer (1999); and *Military Buttons of the American Revolution* by Don Troiani (2001). Every one of these books has value, and it is important to remember that collectors, reenactors, and other types of historians frequently have special expertise that archeologists do not have in one or more areas of material culture.

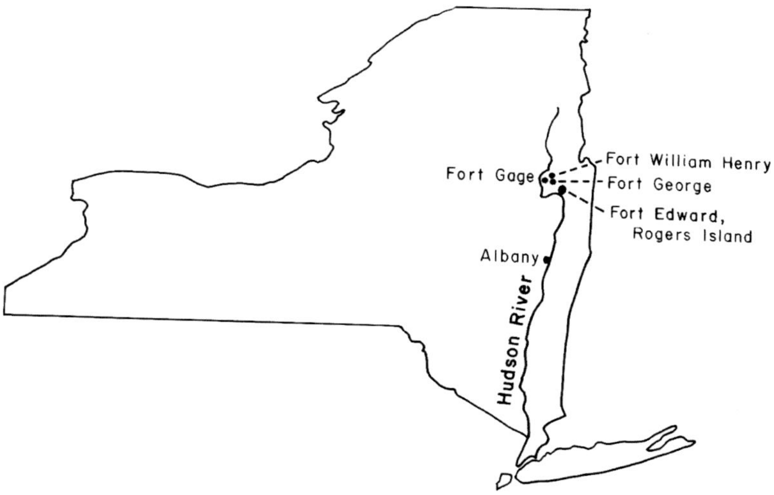

FIG. 1.2. Military sites in Fort Edward and Lake George, New York. "Lake George" refers both to the body of water located at the southeastern corner of the Adirondack Mountains and to the modern village on the southern shore of the lake.

Material culture studies are sometimes highly quantitative (especially so with site reports and cultural resource management studies), but there is a growing literature that successfully combines scholarship with aesthetically pleasing artifact photography. These include *Keys to the Past: Archaeological Treasures of Mackinac* by Lynn Evans (2003); *"A Soldier-Like Way": The Material Culture of the British Infantry 1751–1768* by R. R. Gale (2007); *"Come all you Gallant Heroes": The World of the Revolutionary Soldier* by the Sons of the Revolution in the State of New York (1991); and *Legacy of the Machault: A Collection of 18th-Century Artifacts* by Catherine Sullivan (1986). Both *Keys to the Past* and *Legacy of the Machault* are especially effective, and artifacts pictured in *Legacy of the Machault* are organized around some of the central focuses of life, such as "Commerce and Trade," "Weaponry," "Tools and Equipment," "Food and Drink," and "Clothing." Both Fort Michilimackinac and the *Machault* overlap in time with the military camps in Fort Edward and Lake George, and this volume on artifacts of the British armies is organized in much the same way, hopefully revealing regional preferences and sometimes the inability to obtain certain supplies.

History of the Colonial Wars in Northern New York

The British movement into northeastern New York in the mid-eighteenth century was opposed by France, which had already made competing claims to the same region. Some years earlier, between 1734 and 1737, the French had constructed Fort St. Frederic on Lake Champlain, but hostilities escalated further with the clash between the French and British at the Battle of Lake George, at the southern end of that lake. When Sir William Johnson fought and defeated a French army led by the Baron Dieskau, a direct result was the construction of the first substantial British forts in the region: Fort William Henry at the south end of Lake George and Fort Edward on the Hudson River, approximately thirteen miles to the south. The French, for their part, responded by constructing Fort Carillon (Ticonderoga) where it overlooked the route from Lake Champlain to Lake George, and both sides began to seasonally shift large forces into the region. In the years that followed, both empires created sizeable encampments—essentially cities on the frontier—that today's archeologists are able to study.

On the British side, the histories of Fort William Henry and Fort Edward were intertwined from the beginning. In 1755, bastioned forts were constructed at both sites, adopting the designs of the innovative French designer of forts, the Marquis de Vauban, Sébastien Le Prestre. These were superior to any fortifications that the British had previously introduced to their American colonies. The fort in Fort Edward was much larger and inherently safer because it was farther from the French forts in the north, whereas Fort William Henry was much more exposed to enemy attack. Sir William Johnson, General Jeffrey Amherst, Major General James Abercromby, and thousands of soldiers and officers marched or rode back and forth between these two forts, turning each settlement at times into one of the largest population centers in the colonies. However, what has survived archeologically in the two communities is rather different. Larger, more permanent encampment sites exist in the town of Fort Edward, which never witnessed a major battle and which has had less disturbance from modern development. In contrast, the well-known tourist destination of Lake George features the site of Fort William Henry, scene of a prominent battle and of the most infamous massacre of the French and Indian War, as well as several less well-known forts and extensive military encampments. Sites in Fort Edward may thus provide better insights into how daily life was conducted at a military camp, whereas the ruins of Fort William Henry may be better suited to providing information about warfare and siege tactics.

At these twin bases, British armies drilled as a prelude to attacking the French forts on Lake Champlain. The encampment in Fort Edward consisted of a massive log fort on the east side of the Hudson River, surrounded by an extensive "tent city," and with an equally large settlement on Rogers Island in the middle of the river (fig. 1.3). Fort Edward was also home to a total of eight blockhouses and a sutlers' (merchants') camp of civilians. (The sutlers are discussed in chapter 2.) Rogers Island and Fort Edward both had several general hospitals for treating soldiers from throughout the north country, and the island had a smallpox hospital as well. After the Treaty of Paris ended the French and Indian War in 1763, Rogers Island and

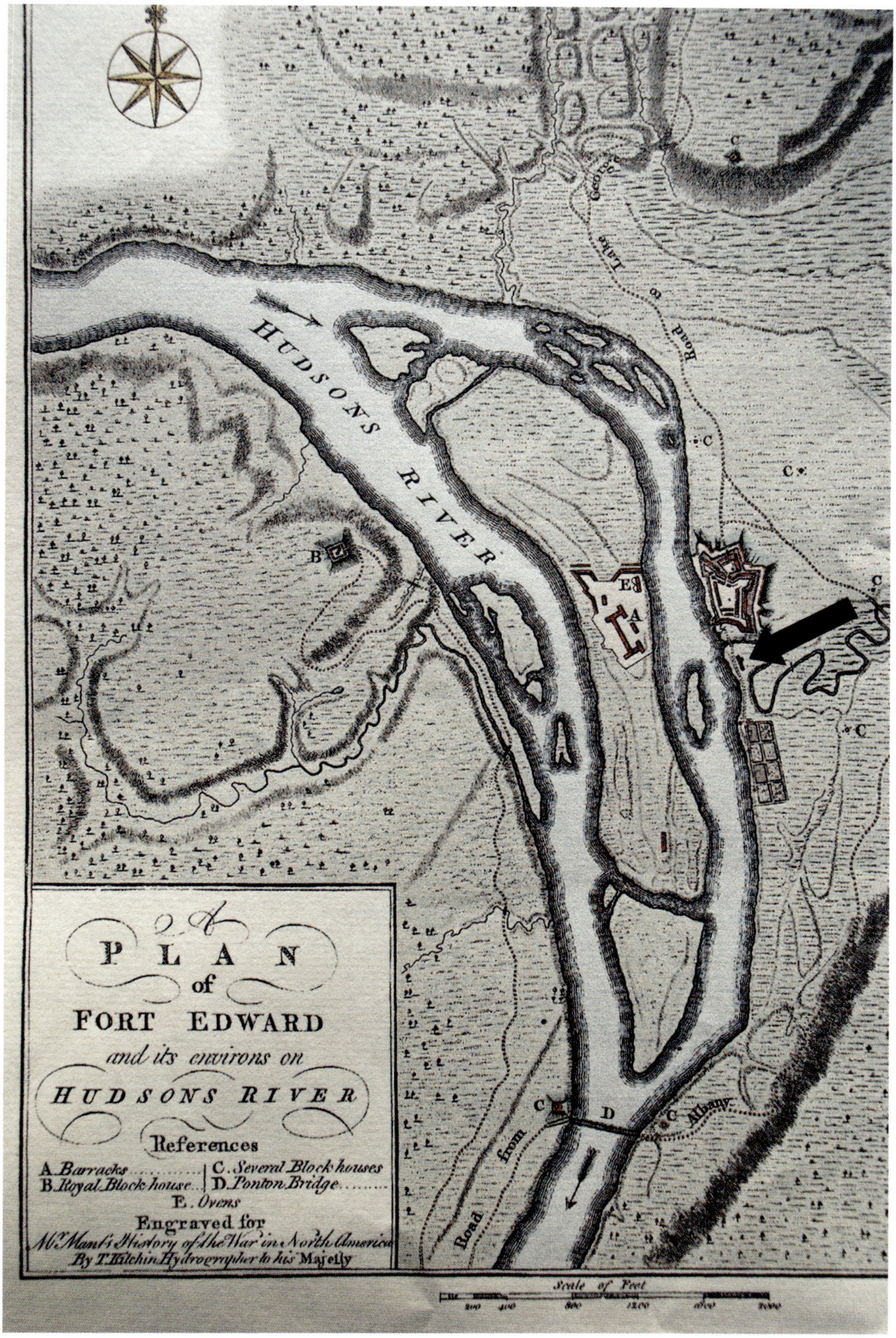

FIG. 1.3. *A Plan of Fort Edward and its environs on Hudsons River*. Engraved for Thomas Mante, 1772, by T. Kitchen, hydrographer to His Majesty. A black arrow has been added to indicate the location of the main sutling camp. *Catalog of Kings Maps, British Museum*

Fort Edward were occupied by very few soldiers up until the Revolution, at which time some of the buildings were reoccupied. After both wars were over, the modern village of Fort Edward slowly grew up over the ruins of the fort for the next 200 years, but most of Rogers Island was never built upon. The result was a community that today has relatively good preservation of many archeological sites, including the remains of barracks buildings, huts, tents, storehouses, kilns, and hospitals.

Turning to Lake George, the garrison at Fort William Henry surrendered to a numerically superior force of French and Indians on August 9, 1757, and the fort was then burned and never built upon again (Steele 1990; Starbuck 2002). In the following year, the British built a small fort, Fort Gage, on high ground to the southwest, and then in July of 1759, General Jeffrey Amherst selected a hilltop overlooking the south end of Lake George and commenced the construction of a much larger fortification, Fort George. Located within what is now the Lake George Battlefield Park, this hilltop had also been the location of the earlier Battle of Lake George and of an entrenched camp that held 1,800 British soldiers and militia during the defense of Fort William Henry in 1757 (fig. 1.4).

Fort George briefly became the principal northern base from which to attack the French, but the fort was rendered unnecessary after Amherst's victory at Ticonderoga in the summer of 1759. Only the southwest bastion of this stone fort was ever completed, but the British did construct a smaller wooden stockade of three bastions, along with barracks, hospitals, storehouses, and other buildings. Dozens of structures covered this hilltop, and the huge British base was still lightly garrisoned in 1775 when Americans under Captain Bernard Romans captured the fort. Fort George subsequently became the base for the largest concentration of smallpox hospitals in North America; two to three thousand soldiers were sent there after the disastrous American invasion of Canada at the end of 1775. Today depressions and foundation stones from dozens of military buildings are still visible from the British and American military encampments that stood there in the 1750s and 1770s, overshadowed by the southwest bastion of Fort George, which has seen extensive stabilization efforts over the years.

The History of Military Sites Archeology in Northeastern New York State

The northeastern corner of New York State played only a modest role in the development of the field of historical archeology, although William Calver and Reginald Bolton did considerable artifact collecting at eighteenth-century military sites in the region (Calver and Bolton 1950; Starbuck 1999a).

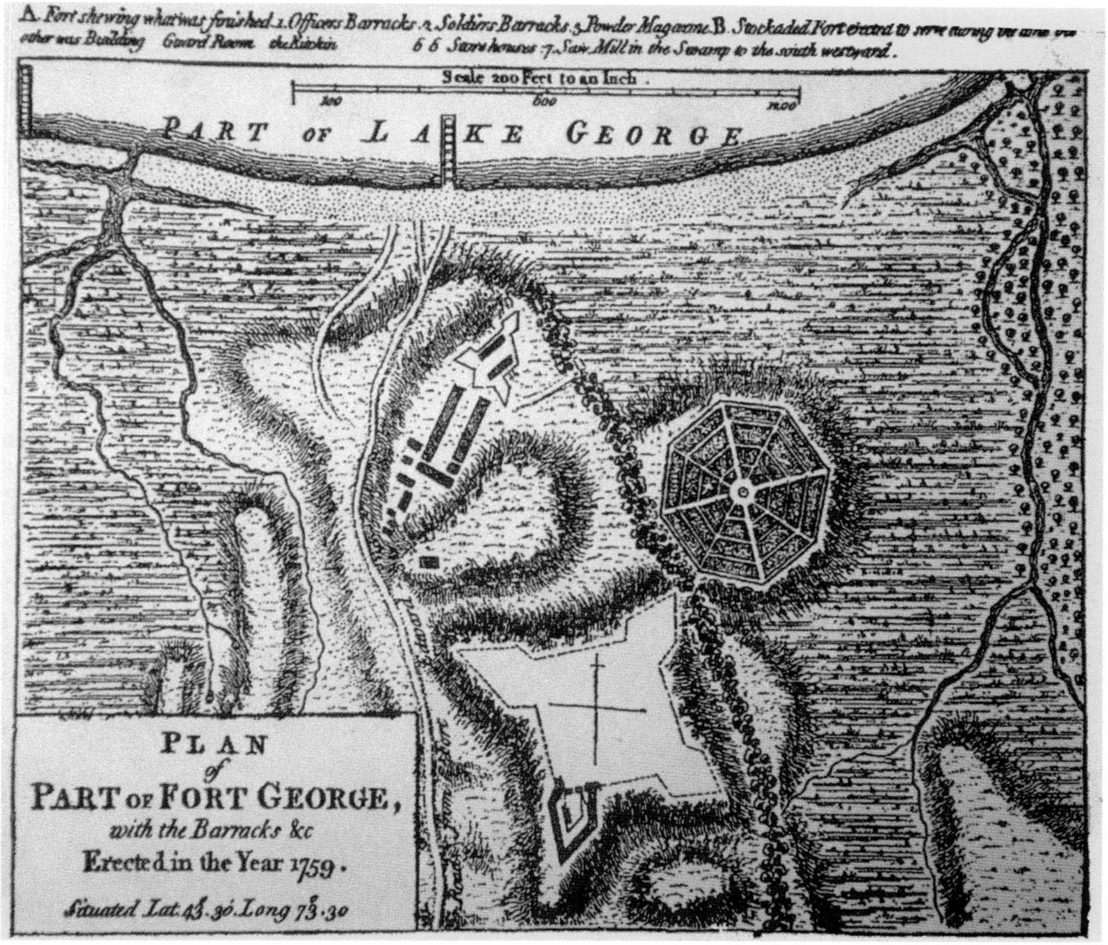

FIG. 1.4. *Plan of Part of Fort George, with the Barracks &c Erected in the year 1759. Courtesy of the Fort William Henry Corporation*

However, more serious research began in the early 1950s when Stanley Gifford conducted a semi-professional excavation at Fort William Henry (Gifford 1955). Gifford, employed by the developers who were reconstructing that fort, completely excavated the northwest bastion of the fort's ruins, but no excavation records have survived. A few years later, another semi-professional excavation was conducted, this time by Duncan Campbell at the remains of the French Village at Fort Ticonderoga (Campbell 1958). This was followed in the late 1960s by the "pick and shovel archeologist," Roland Robbins, who was employed by New York State in digging the ruins of the British and French forts at Crown Point and Fort St. Frederic (Robbins and Jones 1959:chapter 13).

After this slow beginning, the first professional military sites archeology in the region was the excavation of Fort Gage in Lake George Village in 1975. At that time Paul Huey and Lois Feister directed a rescue excavation at the remains of the 1758 fort prior to the construction of a motel (Feister and Huey 1985). Earthworks, the northwest bastion of the fort, and a moat around the fort were all still visible at the time, but nearly all traces of the fort were removed after their salvage effort. Later, they went on to conduct several professional excavations at "His Majesty's Fort of Crown Point" (Feister 1984a, 1984b).

Looking back on that period, it may be that professional excavations were slow to begin in northern New York State because of the perception that "real" archeologists worked on Native American sites, whereas military sites were thought to be well documented already. The irony in this, of course, is that some very good military sites archeology was already taking place elsewhere. Sites such as Fort Ligonier and Fort Necessity in Pennsylvania, Fort Michilimackinac in the Upper Peninsula of Michigan, and Fortress Louisbourg in Nova Scotia were all undergoing extensive excavations, and those projects were all resulting in some excellent publications (Grimm 1970; Stone 1974; Harrington 1957; Fry 1984).

Archeological Sites in Fort Edward

Rogers Island

Rogers Island was the centerpiece of the largest British encampment of the French and Indian War, some fifteen to sixteen thousand British soldiers in the late 1750s. Coupled with the fort in Fort Edward and the extensive settlements on the east bank of the Hudson River, this was a formidable position from which to drive the French out of northern New York. For thirty years Rogers Island was owned by Earl Stott, an amateur historian who loved Rogers' Rangers, the irregular military forces that made Rogers Island their home. Over the space of thirty years, Stott successfully persuaded a few thousand volunteers to dig with him, and he did far more than any other person to demonstrate that there is a great deal of military history still lying in the ground in northern New York State. His volunteer helpers excavated thousands of musket balls, belt axes, bayonets, and even an intact brass compass from Rogers Island (Rogers Island Historical Association 1986). Stott was charming, enthusiastic, and loved telling stories about the Rangers. Unfortunately, nothing from his extensive artifact collection is currently stored or displayed in Fort Edward.

Stott eventually sold Rogers Island to developers, who hired me in 1991 to begin digging on Rogers Island prior to the possible construction of a private marina. Between 1991 and 1994, and again from 1997 to 1998, my archeological team from Adirondack Community College excavated massive brick fireplaces inside a large barracks building on the island; smaller fireplaces inside the remains of tents and crude cabins; most of a large storehouse building; many dumps; and a garbage-filled latrine that contained axes, buttons, musket balls, and thousands of butchered animal bones. From this archeology, we learned many small details about the lives of Rangers and Regulars: for example, that they built rough, temporary shelters for themselves; chiefly ate meat from cows and pigs; made their own musket balls; wore extremely plain, undecorated buttons and buckles; and led a fairly spartan existence (Starbuck 1995, 1997a, 2004).

Undeniably our most significant discovery was at the southern end of Rogers Island, where we uncovered the outline of the camp's smallpox hospital, positioned hundreds of feet from the main encampment. The dump next to the smallpox hospital was one of the many artifact-rich deposits on Rogers Island that we were able to study over the years (Starbuck 1997b).

The Fort in Fort Edward

The remains of the largest British fort of the French and Indian War now lie underneath several streets and many yards of the modern community of Fort Edward. Most homeowners on Moon, Edward, and Old Fort streets have small artifact collections, generally found when the cellars were dug for their houses, but there is one outstanding collection of artifacts obtained early in the town's history: the McDougall Collection, owned by the Fort Edward Historical Association, Inc. This collection derives from the home of William McDougall, who lived on Moon Street in "what must have been about the center of the site of the old fort" (Hill 1956). McDougall liked to hire boys to dig on his property, but given the nature of this collecting, it is not possible to associate these artifacts with any specific historic structure or activity area. Still, they do appear to span every fort activity imaginable, and some of these artifacts are really quite exceptional, including a halberd, inscribed razor handles, a copper skillet, a pewter cup, bayonets, spades, axes, buckles, musket parts, buttons, hinges, pole tips, gunflints, ice creepers, ox shoes, wagon wheel rims, and even a sizeable lead ingot (not yet melted to form musket balls). This collection is definitely of "exhibit quality," and over the years it has been on display in several locations in Fort Edward (currently in the Rogers Island Visitors Center).

The surface of Fort Edward today gives few clues to what might lie underneath, but from 1995 to 1996 and from 2002 to 2004 we excavated pits throughout several of the lawns that now cover Fort Edward, and we even dug inside the cellar of one house. In the process we found charred timbers from structures that once stood inside the fort, as well as evidence for the

FIG. 1.5. Ongoing laboratory work at Plymouth State University. Amanda Allen (on the right) is sorting and reassembling tobacco pipes from the Fort Edward sutling house, and Elizabeth Hall (far left) has been overseeing the laboratory analysis.

eastern and western edges of the fort. Most of the artifacts were extremely fragmentary, suggesting that scavenging by homeowners or collectors had removed anything of size, but we did find part of the bowl from a Micmac pipe and a bone whistle or flute (see fig. 9.4 and Starbuck 2004:99).

Fort Edward is the last truly major British fort of the French and Indian War that is still uninterpreted and on private land, and it is our hope that eventually some of the modern houses might be cleared from its surface, allowing it to be protected and interpreted as a fort. Drawing upon artifacts from both the McDougall Collection and our own recent work, there would be ample artifacts to display there.

The Sutling Camp in Fort Edward

The most recent excavation in Fort Edward has been at the site of a sutling house that once stood on the east bank of the Hudson River, just south of where the 1755 fort was constructed. The sutling house and its contents are discussed in detail in chapter 2, and the analysis of the sutlers' artifacts is ongoing, both at the Rogers Island Visitors Center and at Plymouth State University (fig. 1.5).

Archeological Sites in Lake George

Fort William Henry: The 1950s

It was in 1953 that Stanley Gifford was hired to take charge of the full-scale excavation of Fort William Henry as a prelude to reconstruction. Gifford's work focused on locating the outlines of key buildings, finding the fort's cemetery, and recovering artifacts suitable for exhibits. His dig included sizeable portions of the fort, as well as dumps outside the fort, and an enormous assemblage of artifacts was recovered from the ruins (Starbuck 1991, 1993). Many of these are still either on display or in storage at the reconstructed fort. While Gifford left no excavation report behind, nevertheless there is an extensive card catalog that documents the artifact collection.

Most of these materials date to the French and Indian War, and historical sources describe no efforts by later armies to camp on top of the fort's ruins, given the stigma attached to the surrender and massacre. Unavoidably, there are some nineteenth- and twentieth-century artifacts included in the fort's exhibits and collections. This is hardly surprising, given the fort's popularity as a tourist destination throughout all time periods. Of the many thousands of artifacts, there are great numbers of nails, spikes, hinges, fragments of charred wood, many exploded mortar shells, much lead buckshot, bayonets, spades, axes, hoes, tobacco pipes, ox shoes, horseshoes, bits of lead sprue, iron tips from poles, and smaller numbers of pottery sherds, Jew's harps, ice creepers, and more. While spectacular, the collection reflects the period in which it was excavated—the 1950s—and there are few butchered animal bones or other ecofacts. Also, because sifting screens were seldom used at that time, many of the smaller artifacts from inside the fort's ruins may not have been recovered.

Fort William Henry: The 1990s

No excavations took place at the fort between 1957 and 1997, except in the fort's cemetery (Liston and Baker 1995), but between 1997 and 2000 my team from Adirondack Community College conducted four summer field schools both inside and outside the reconstructed fort (Starbuck 1998, 2002b, 2008b). Inside the fort we opened up sizeable areas of the parade ground, where we sometimes descended for eight feet or more inside the

FIG. 1.6. The excavation of a cellar room within the West Barracks at Fort William Henry.

cellars of former buildings. Much of our time was spent shoring up sandy walls with two-by-eights and sheets of plywood as we tried to prevent the inevitable collapses. Fort William Henry was built on a glacial lake terrace above Lake George, and the pit walls caved in constantly!

Among other things, we dug the original stone-lined well for the fort, at the north end of the parade ground. The well had been dug by Rogers' Rangers in 1756, and the upper part had been partially excavated in the late 1950s. When excavated in 1997, we discovered that the well extended to a depth of about thirty feet. At the very bottom, underneath tourist artifacts, pinecones, and the detritus of two hundred and fifty years, we found a dozen lead musket balls, four French gunflints, nine small pieces of lead (probably sewn as weights into the fringe of a garment), and a base fragment from a square-sided case bottle (Starbuck 2001).

On the western side of the parade ground, our excavation inside the foundation of the West Barracks was extensive, and we exposed more than fifty feet of the West Barracks' east wall. Excavations revealed about twenty feet of burned timbers in the bottom of one trench, and we found large postholes alongside (sometimes still retaining the bases of large posts). We even discovered a small room outlined with charred timbers, measuring just five feet by six feet (fig. 1.6), as well as the imposing stone base of a barracks fireplace. The artifacts found inside the West Barracks foundation included buttons, buckles, cufflinks, a finger ring, a broken bayonet, the stem from a wine glass, a delft (tin-glazed earthenware) ointment jar, gaming pieces of lead, the corner of a sharpening stone, the base from a case bottle, the delicate bone inlay from the handle of a knife, a pair of scissors, a small brass spoon, at least two fish hooks, and thousands of burned fragments of animal bones. And throughout the foundation we found exploded mortar shell fragments and cannister shot, as well as musket balls and gunflints. While many of the pieces of mortar shells may be French, lobbed over the walls into the fort, some were no doubt British shells that had blown apart prematurely. We also found sewing supplies in the ruins of the barracks, including a thimble, a needle, and eighteen straight pins.

Our archeology outside the reconstructed fort chiefly focused upon the dump east of the fort, culminating in 1999 with the construction of a huge trench running up the side of the modern slope. As the trench approached the wall of the fort, cultural deposits became deeper, and diggers at the bottom of the trench were unearthing artifacts at eleven and twelve feet below today's surface. Our artifact sample from just this one dump included nearly sixteen thousand fragments of butchered bones, many musket balls (seventy-five), British gunflints (thirty-five), French gunflints (thirty-two), metal buttons (thirty-five), cufflinks (three), buckles (five), British halfpence, a Spanish real, two Jew's harps, many hundreds of pottery sherds, and hundreds of fragments of wine bottles.

Fort Gage

The artifacts recovered at Fort Gage by Paul Huey, Lois Feister, and members of the Auringer–Seelye Chapter of the New York State Archaeological Association were not photographed for this volume, but some of the best artifacts appear in Feister and Huey (1985). They include a brass Jew's harp, canteen and bottle fragments, tobacco pipes, musket balls, gunflints, buttons, and more. The artifacts are presently curated by the Bureau of Historic Sites, New York State Office of Parks, Recreation, and Historic Preservation.

Encampment West of Route 9, Vicinity of Birch Avenue

In 1993 I was fortunate to meet with a skilled metal-detector operator who had assembled a large collection of military artifacts (all metal) from the woods west of Route 9 at the south end of the village of Lake George. I pho-

FIG. 1.7. The excavation of the northernmost barracks foundation (probably once occupied by officers) at the Lake George Battlefield Park.

tographed the artifacts (which included cannonballs, chewed musket balls, gunflints, axes, pewter spoons, buttons, buckles, and more), and soon after that an extensive and meticulous rescue excavation was conducted there between 1993 and 1996 by a crew led by Sarah Majot, then the Project Director for Collamer & Associates (Majot 1993, 1994, 1995). In the 1750s this had been the location, at different times, for a Rangers encampment, British Regulars, and French gun emplacements. The many artifacts recovered by the cultural resource investigations included a lancet kit, a canteen and many canteen fragments, a spade, a Jew's harp, grapeshot, gun spalls, musket balls of all sizes (including 52 caliber), a strike-a-light, lock plates, axes, a Spanish real, British half-pence, an ox shoe, finials, and lead sprue (Sarah Majot, personal communication, February 14, 2009).

Lake George Battlefield Park

In 2000 and 2001 I received permission from the New York State Department of Environmental Conservation to conduct the first professional archeology in Lake George Battlefield Park. We spent the two summers sampling the remains from an amazing variety of military buildings, some of which are among the most intact in our region (Starbuck 2002; Vandrei 2001). In the summer of 2000 we dug with crews into the clearly visible foundations of two of the barracks buildings that General Amherst had ordered to be constructed there in 1759. In the process, we discovered well-preserved walls and numerous artifacts from both the French and Indian War and the American Revolution. These were located inside the previously mentioned wooden stockade with three bastions, at the northern edge of the bluff that overlooks the southern end of Lake George. From engineers' maps prepared in the 1750s, we knew that this wooden fortification had contained two small barracks buildings and was the front line of defense while the main fort, Fort George, was being constructed about six hundred feet to the south.

The more northerly of these foundations measured seventeen by sixty-seven feet, and inside we discovered great quantities of fallen wall plaster, suggesting that it may have been an officers' barracks (fig. 1.7). The second foundation, less finished in appearance, may have housed the enlisted men. We also found thousands of pottery sherds and animal bones from the soldiers' meals, including fish bones from Lake George, and many buttons—some of which were numbered regimental buttons from the Revolutionary War—plus a four-pound cannonball, musket parts, hinges, wine bottles, medicine bottles, a spade, a single strip of gold braid from a uniform, and even the hinge from a chest that bore the inscribed name of a possible officer, "Ahmuty."

During the 2001 season we examined a larger sample of huts and barracks and even placed several test pits inside the one surviving bastion of Fort George. Once again we relied very heavily upon British engineers' maps of the late 1750s, and these helped lead us to the foundations of at least eight or ten additional buildings. We sampled each of these with small numbers of pits, and also tested some of the dumps and earthworks. Each feature had been drawn on the 1750s maps, but each also contained numbered regimental buttons and sherds of creamware that would not have been in use until the Revolution.

The most distinctive artifacts that we recovered in 2001 included a well-preserved brass pocket sundial and compass with the Roman numerals "XXIX" scratched onto the case, probably indicating that the British 29th Regiment of Foot (which fought at the Battle of Saratoga) had carried, and lost, what must have been a valuable compass. We also found the ruptured barrel from a British "Brown Bess" musket, a lead weight, buttons of the British 26th Regiment, stems from wine glasses, an intact door-lock mechanism, a complete bayonet, and two very fine stock clasps of brass.

Archeological sites within the Lake George Battlefield Park have exceptionally high integrity, and the park has seen very little digging over the years, thanks to careful management and protection by the New York State Department of Environmental Conservation. Some of the artifacts recovered in 2000–2001 were subsequently conserved by the Lake Champlain Maritime Museum, using funds raised by the Lake George Battlefield Park (Fort George) Alliance, and all materials are now being curated by the New York State Museum in Albany.

"This Day I Workd for Mr Best[.] First went to Work on His Seller [Cellar] on ye Small Island."
—Jabez Fitch, Jr.
(June 4, 1757)

2

The Sutling House in Fort Edward

The Crucial Source of Supplies

EXCAVATIONS at military sites have had tremendous success in revealing information about soldiers and officers far from home as they waited to fight, drilled, hunted and fished, and spent time socializing, dining, smoking, and drinking at their campsites. Fighters, yes, but they must also be viewed as consumers. Their provisions were largely provided from military storehouses, but most encampments welcomed additional supplies sold by the sutlers attached to each camp.

Sutlers are the civilian merchants who live alongside military camps and sell goods to the army. These sales have gone on for hundreds, probably thousands, of years. For officers and soldiers who had traveled far from home in the eighteenth century, "regular issue," including such things as salt beef, salt pork, dried peas, dried beans, and a modest supply of rum, probably wasn't very interesting. Still, substantial profits were no doubt available to those who could sell some niceties, or some vices, to the soldiers. Private contractors could provide extra alcohol, tobacco, coffee, tea, chocolate, sugar, cloth, replacements for missing or broken dishes, buttons, and probably much more to soldiers and officers who had the means.

Given the ubiquitous nature of sutlers' camps, it is perhaps surprising that more have not been dug by archeologists. Supplies storehouses have been dug, notably the log provision storehouse built at Fort Michilimackinac in 1780, later dug by Roger Grange in the 1980s (Grange 1987). Historical research has also been conducted on army sutlers, most notably by David Delo (1998), although that work chiefly deals with Western army posts throughout the nineteenth century. But did sutlers' camps and sutling houses of the mid-eighteenth century sell supplies that were *different* from regular issue? We do know from historical sources that they sold to soldiers and officers, under agreement with the army, and that their business practices and prices were tightly monitored by regimental commanders. As noted by Delo,

> At Fort Edward . . . all of the sutlers in camp were licensed, even though permission to suttle did not guarantee that a sutler would be attached to a regiment. And like bachelors, unattached sutlers were camped together. No sutler was to pitch his tent or break ground or build a hut . . . without first applying to the Adjutant Deputy Quartermaster General, under penalty of having all liquor and stores demolished. . . . Order and discipline in the camp were enforced by the provost guard. No lights were allowed at night, and soldiers were not allowed in the sutlers' area after retreat. (1998:9)

Goods were sold at fixed prices, and the power to enforce or reduce prices was held by the commanding officer. While sutlers' merchandise only infrequently appeared in lists of provisions, there are a few historical listings that reference some of the supplies that were being sold in Fort Edward (Hill 1929:180):

> Under date of the 18th, [Col. William] Henshaw notes the following purchases from a Mr. Forsey, evidently a camp sutler. They are of interest, as they show the class of articles sold by these merchants and the prices prevailing at the time.

	York Currency
A tea pot	8 sh. – 0 d
1 – 2 lb. of tea @ 12 – 6 pound	6 " – 3 "
2 lbs. sugar @ 1 – 6 pound	3 " – 0 "
3 cups and saucers	2 " – 6 "
1 cake chocolate	3 " – 6 "
2 lbs. sugar	3 " – 0 "
1 spoon, 1 sh. –2 quarts of milk 8d	1 " – 8 "
	£ 1 – 7 – 11

On the 5th of July he bought from a Mr. Cutler the following:

1 piece of nankeen (cloth)	1 – 2 – 0
2 dozen buttons: 18d. dozen	3 – 0
Thread	1 – 0
	£ 1 – 6 – 0

Col. Henshaw later purchased additional sewing supplies (Henshaw 1909: 221):

> Thursday the 9th of Augt. 1759 Bought of Mess. Cutler & Brewer –

	s d
4 & ½ Yds. Of Green Batteen @ 10/ P yd.	£ 2 – 5 – 0
3 & ½ Yds. Of Shalloon @ 4/ P Yd.	14 –

3 Sticks of Mohair @ 6d Each	1 – 6
2 hanks of Green Silk @ 1/ Each	2 –
½ Yd. Buckram @ 3/ P Yd.	1 – 6
Green thread 6d. penny Worth	– 6
2 Dozn. of Buttons @ 4/2d P Dozn.	8 – 4
Total	£ 3 – 12 – 10

In 1991, when we commenced digging British colonial sites in Fort Edward, New York, our interest was in locating military features and in demonstrating how frontier settings may have led to variations upon standard military practice. But we were digging the *points of consumption*—the huts and tents where there was ample evidence for the food, drink, clothing and armaments that had been purchased and used. At no point did we search for a *point of supply*, exemplified by the sutling houses that sold goods to the army and made life on the frontier a bit more tolerable. A sutling house clearly served as a residence (for the sutler[s] and his employees), as a storehouse, and as a point of sale. Most also doubled as taverns, so an additional goal for us was to look for evidence of unusually large numbers of drinking vessels, serving dishes, or cutlery. The soldier Jabez Fitch, Jr., wrote in his diary on September 21, 1757, "In ye Morning Serjt Comstoc Samll Billings & I went to ye Setlers [sutlers] & Drinkd Som Rhum" (Fitch, Jr. 1968:26), and this reinforces the popular assumption that most sutling houses were drinking establishments. The consumption of alcohol, however, was governed by the following regulations: "No Person Belonging to the Garrison or Hospital to stay at any of the Sutlers after Night fall under the pain of being Severly punished & any Sutler that Entertains them after Night fall shall have his Liquor Spilt—& he shall be Drummed out from the Garrison" (Henshaw 1909:234).

Because Fort Edward was home to the largest British military encampment of the French and Indian War, there were literally thousands of consumers residing there with relatively few choices as to where they might purchase supplies. The most likely scenario is that goods were transported up the Hudson River from Albany, unloaded on the riverbank, and probably exchanged for cash on the next payday. Of the several engineers' maps that were prepared for Fort Edward in the 1750s, the earliest ones—from 1755 (fig. 2.1) and 1756 (fig. 2.2)—do not yet show any sutling houses. Later maps do, and these were sometimes drawn as one long building, sometimes two (fig. 2.3), and by 1760, two clusters of buildings, with three buildings in each cluster (fig. 2.4). All of these were nestled on a point of high ground between a bend of Little Wood Creek and the east bank of the Hudson River, just south of the modern village of Fort Edward. The sutlers' camp was positioned very close to the British Army (just a few hundred feet

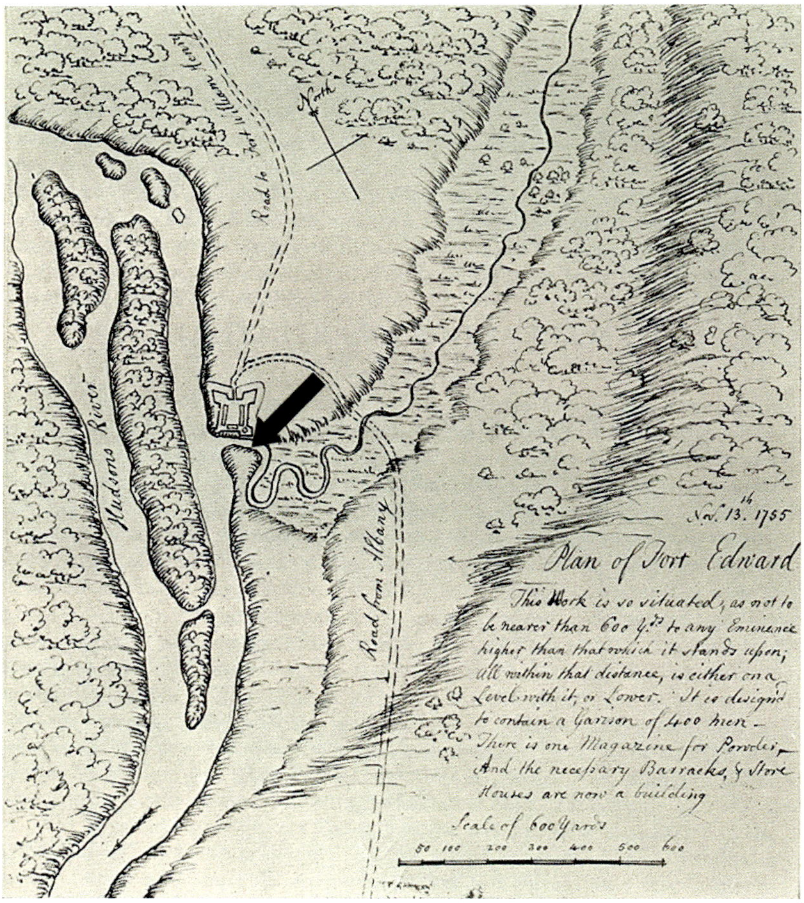

FIG. 2.1. Map of Fort Edward, 1755. The black arrow has been added to indicate where the sutling house was later constructed. *Crown Collection of Photographs of American Maps, New York State Library*

from the fort), yet its commercial function set it apart. Also, it appears there was a separate sutlers' camp on Rogers Island, even though we do not have a historical map showing us exactly where. With each regiment having its own sutler, there may easily have been dozens of sutlers stationed in Fort Edward during the war.

As of 1732, there already had been a prominent trading establishment in Fort Edward, the trading post of John Henry Lydius, a Dutchman from Albany who traded with Indians throughout northern New York and into eastern Canada (Hamilton 1964). While his principal building was probably positioned on the higher river terrace to the north, where Fort Edward was later constructed, he may well have placed his storehouses in the same area where the sutlers later camped, and some of his buildings may have been reused by the sutlers of the 1750s.

Soldiers' diaries in Fort Edward make occasional references to buying supplies from sutlers, and a "Mr. Best" and a "Mr. Pommery" were among

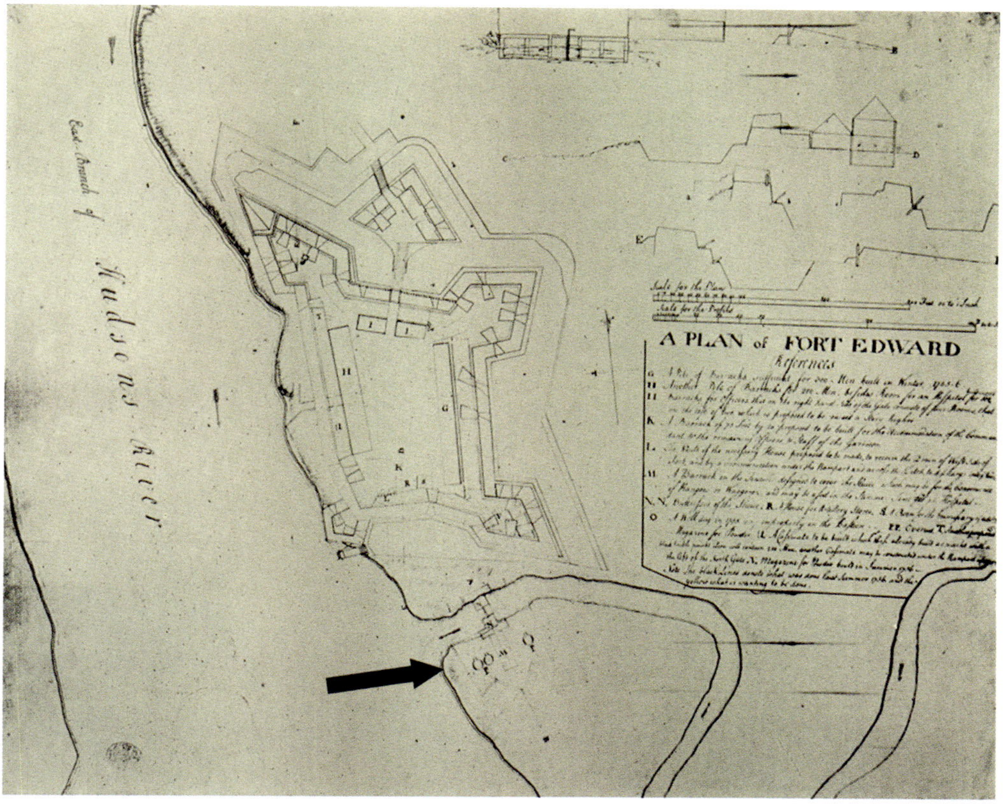

FIG. 2.2. Plan of Fort Edward, 1756. The black arrow has been added to point to ovens and a barracks that were constructed prior to the sutling house. *Crown Collection of Photographs of American Maps, New York State Library*

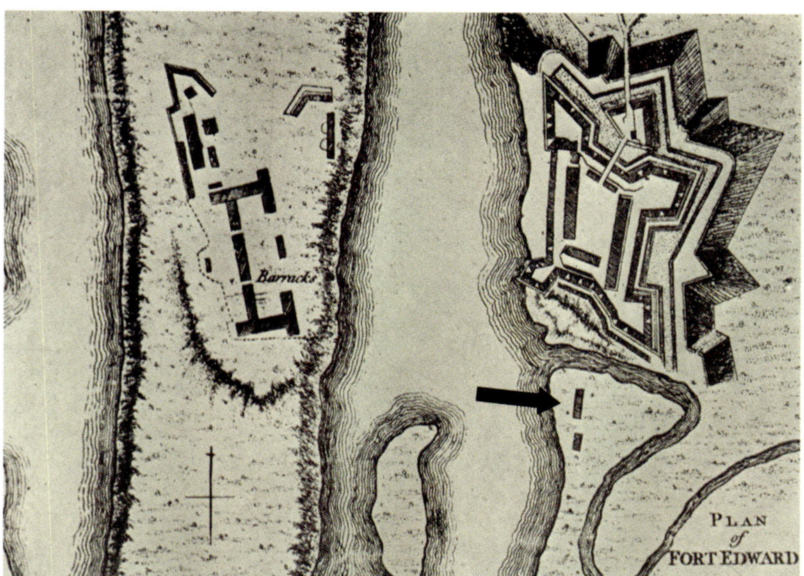

FIG. 2.3. Plan of Fort Edward, undated. The black arrow has been added to point to the more northerly of two sutling houses, the house where excavations have been conducted since 2001. *Crown Collection of Photographs of American Maps, New York State Library*

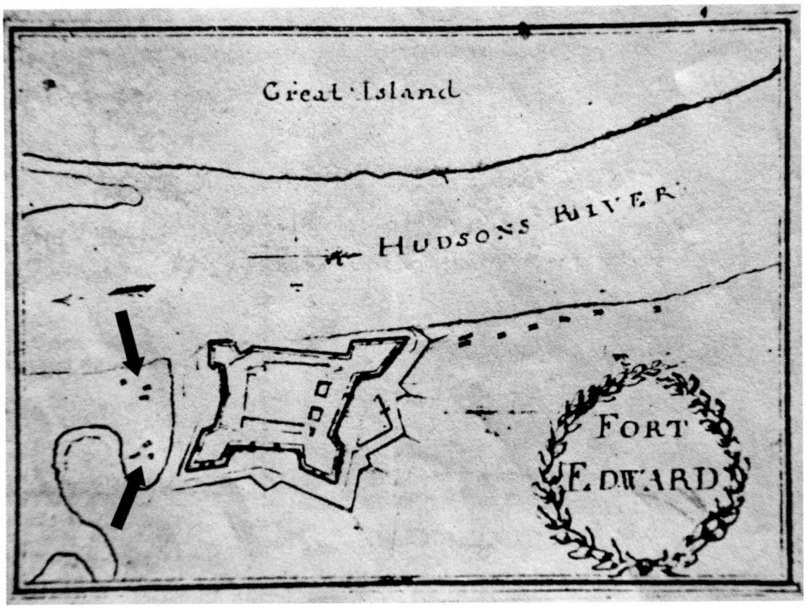

FIG. 2.4. Map of Fort Edward, 1760. The upper black arrow points to a cluster of sutling houses on the east bank of the Hudson River, the area where we have conducted our excavations. The lower black arrow identifies a second cluster of sutling houses, not visible on any other map. Testing in 2004 found a thin artifact scatter in the more southerly area, but no direct evidence for buildings. *Crown Collection of Photographs of American Maps, New York State Library*

those who provisioned the troops. Mr. Best built his home and a storehouse just south of the fort in 1757, and Jabez Fitch, Jr., makes several references to getting "pickets" (probably temporary fencing) for Mr. Best (Fitch, Jr. 1968); also, "Mr Best Treted Me with a Dram of Cordial" (Fitch, Jr. 1968:3), and "I went over to Mr Bests & Drinkd Some Jenava" (Fitch, Jr. 1968:10). Fitch's references to Mr. Pommery are even more specific, and on June 6, 1757, he mentioned "Mr. Pummery our Setler [sutler] Came Up with His Stores" (1968:10); on July 10, 1757, he described, "I Got Some Suger at Pummerys [Pommery] for Mix" (1968:11); and on December 3, 1757, he "Met Pumroy [Pommery] ye Setler who was Going Home" (1968:36). Unfortunately, at no point does Fitch mention exactly where Pommery's sutling house was located, and, given the size of the fort and the encampment in Fort Edward, there no doubt were additional, unnamed sutlers engaged in commerce with the army. This is also suggested by Fitch's statement on November 4, 1757, that "I went over ye River to a Setlers [Sutlers] & Bought a Stick of Mohair to Make My Coat" (Fitch, Jr. 1968:31).

Two years later (1759), General Jeffrey Amherst ordered the construction of a brewery for spruce beer on this same site (Hill 1929:175):

> June 11th__Spruce beer is to be brewed for the health and convenience of the troops, which will be served at prime cost. Five quarts of molasses will be put into every barrel of spruce beer. Each gallon will cost near three coppers.

We have no historical records describing architectural details for the sutlers' houses, or stating when any sutlers other than Mr. Pommery departed, or revealing what may have happened to their houses after abandonment. But after the conquest of Fort Carillon (Ticonderoga) in 1759, the military camps in Fort Edward were quickly abandoned, and the sutlers no doubt moved on, following the army. There is no evidence that the site of the east-bank sutlers' camp was ever built upon in the centuries that followed, but there is a modest scatter of nineteenth-century whiteware, bricks, and mortar near the surface of the sutling camp, and this suggests dumping from later houses on nearby streets. The raised point of land that encompassed the sutlers' camp is now covered with trees, brush, and poison ivy. Even in the eighteenth century, without the flood-control dams that now maintain the level of the Hudson River, only the most pronounced flooding could possibly have raised water to this level, so its elevation and relative dryness were no doubt factors in the decision to build there.

At the start of our excavations in Fort Edward, we paid scant attention to the sutlers' camp on the east bank, although we often wondered where Lydius's trading post might have been. However, in the 1980s and 1990s the sutlers' site came under attack from treasure hunters. In 1996, a visual inspection of the site by Matthew Rozell, a Hudson Falls history teacher, revealed that the surface of what appeared to be the main sutling house, 240 years old, was already riddled with looters' holes. The largest of these was "(about 5 feet square and perhaps 3 feet deep) [and] actually still had a rotted wooden ladder emerging from it" (Rozell 2002:2). Dark-green wine bottle fragments lay everywhere, and there was even a 1745 Spanish one-real coin lying on the surface (Matthew Rozell, personal communication, 1996). Because we were already focused on the excavation of huts and barracks elsewhere, we did not place a field crew at the sutlers' camp until 2001.

Since then we have spent seven field seasons excavating the filled-in cellar hole of the main sutling house (Starbuck 2007, 2008a). Mid-eighteenth-century artifacts lie scattered across the surrounding high ground, but archeological testing has revealed no other buildings with cellars. Working within what appears to have been the most substantial structure at the sutlers' camp, we have excavated down to the burned timbers and boards that lie scattered across what was once the cellar floor (fig. 2.5). Eighteenth-century artifacts are present at all depths, but on the cellar floor we have found the densest concentrations of artifacts that once filled the building, either as merchandise to be sold or else as the personal belongings of the sutlers themselves. (See the appendix for a summary of these findings.) As the sutling house burned, everything had dropped or settled to the lowermost floor. The burning initially raised the question of whether this might have been one of the Lydius buildings known to have been burned by an expedition of French and Indians after a raid on November 27, 1745 (Hill

FIG. 2.5. Excavating the sutling house in the summer of 2007 (facing southwest). The plastic sheeting and tarpaulins are used to keep stains and features from drying out in the sun.

1929:34–35; Hamilton 1964:272), and then rebuilt or built over by the sutlers.

However, evidence from the diary of Jabez Fitch, Jr., suggests otherwise. On June 4, 1757, Fitch describes:

> This Day I Workd for Mr Best First went to Work on His Seller [Cellar] on ye Small Island In ye afternoon went to Get Som Timber on ye Rode we found Near 40 Cakes of chocalet Spild By Laying in ye Sun at Night I Recd 2S [shillings] For my Days work (Fitch, Jr. 1968:3)

Because we know that "Mr. Best" had located his business south of the fort, this reference to working on a "Seller" [Cellar] in 1757—truly a rarity within the entire Fort Edward encampment—suggests that we have discovered none other than the home and storehouse of Mr. Best. Even more convincing is the reference to "on ye Small Island" because our sutling house would have truly been on an "island" in 1757, surrounded on three sides by Little Wood Creek and on the fourth by the Hudson River.

The journal of Col. James Montresor, a Royal Engineer later known for the construction of Fort George, is equally useful in describing the operation of Mr. Best. Not only does Montresor describe dining "at Best" on June 25, 1757; June 19, 1759; and December 3, 1759 (Scull 1882:17, 77, 109), he also provides a specific reference to some of the spirits that were available for sale:

> Tuesday—July—3rd 1759. Gave Best a permit for 6 Barrels of Rum one Barrel of Jamaica Spirits, one Barrel of Brandy & one of Shrub for the Department of Engineers (Scull 1882:79)

Taken together, the historical references by Jabez Fitch, Jr., and Col. Montresor strongly suggest that our sutling house—Mr. Best's house—was in operation from June of 1757 until at least the end of 1759. This sutling house is truly a time capsule, roughly a two-year window into the essential and profitable commerce that Mr. Best conducted with the British Army.

Luckily, treasure hunting in modern times had caused damage only within the first three to four feet and never extended down to the earth floor at the bottom, which is six to seven feet below the modern ground surface. The cellar was initially hard to interpret, largely because so much dirt had to be removed to obtain a clear view of the floor, but also because historical maps presented too many possibilities. One large building or two? Two

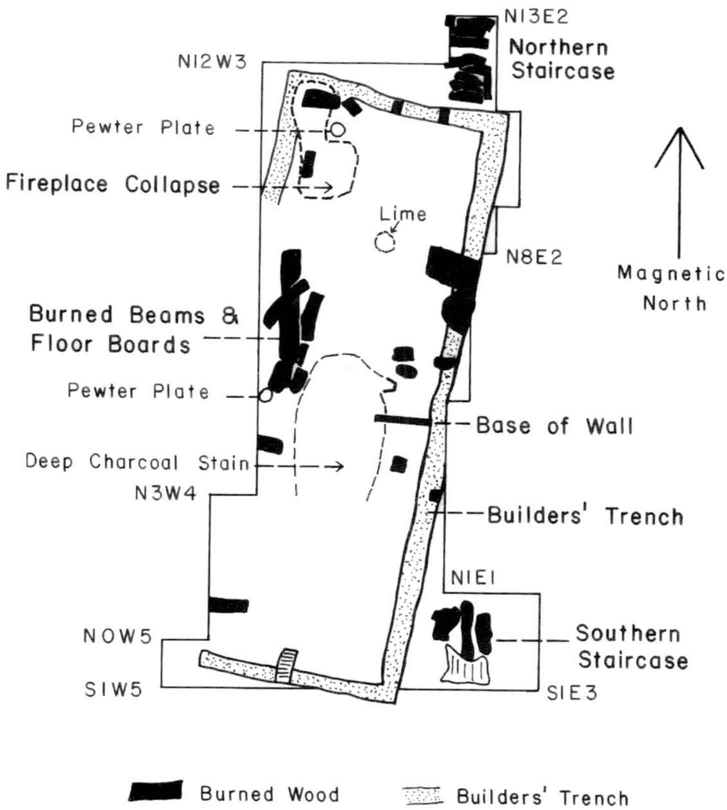

FIG. 2.6. Plan view of the cellar floor of the sutling house, showing the area that was completely excavated, the builders' trench that outlines the former building, postholes (appearing as small black squares) in the cellar floor, and the larger concentrations of burned wood that lie on the cellar floor. The "Fireplace Collapse" in the northwest corner is a pile of bricks from a first-floor fireplace that collapsed down to the cellar floor when the building burned. The origin of the "Deep Charcoal Stain" in the middle of the building is still uncertain, but it appears as a large subfloor feature with many brick fragments and two wrought iron hooks (fig. 6.10) on its western edge.

FIG. 2.7. A dark, linear stain running east–west across the center of the sutling house, all that remains from the base of a wall or door in the middle of the floor (facing east). The meter-long ranging pole that parallels the stain is marked in 10-cm increments.

buildings a short distance apart or connected? Was this frequented only by officers, or was it open to all? And why had the house burned? Was it deliberate, or had a chimney fire prematurely brought the operation to a close?

Early British engineers' maps were contradictory about the camp's layout, and only a broad horizontal exposure, combined with very deep pits, could answer our questions. It was not until the 2007 season that we finally exposed enough to realize that we were looking at the remains of a single fourteen-foot (east–west) by forty-foot (north–south) building (fig. 2.6) with the narrow, linear stain from a wall or door frame still visible across the middle, perfectly bisecting the northern twenty feet of the cellar from the southern twenty feet (fig. 2.7).

The entire house had clearly been consumed by fire, causing some of the artifacts to be burned or melted, and the northern half of the cellar contained many fragments of drinking glasses and wine glasses, delft bowls, white salt-glazed stoneware bowls, cups and saucers, and quite a few bone-handled, two-tined forks and table knives. All of this suggested that the northern half of the sutling house had doubled as a tavern for thirsty and hungry soldiers. But it should not be assumed that spirits were the only drink provided in the tavern. Coffee, tea, and chocolate would all have been extremely popular drinks at this time, and "I would be surprised if [your] tea bowls and saucers or cups did *not* hold chocolate at some point in their working life" (Phil Dunning, personal communication, January 9, 2009). The sutlers probably sold a great deal of hot chocolate, especially in the mornings, and it would have been just as popular as coffee. Historical documentation for the popularity of chocolate as a morning drink is quite good (see Wickman 1997), and the diary of Jabez Fitch, Jr., makes repeated references to consuming chocolate; e.g., on November 14, 1757, "in ye Morning We Made Som Chocalet & Eat it" (Fitch, Jr. 1968:32).

We found large concentrations of bricks at both the northern and southern ends of the house, the remains of fireplaces and chimneys (forty feet apart) that had dropped from the main floor down to the cellar floor when the house burned. A modest number of six- to ten-inch-diameter fieldstones were mixed in with the rubble of the larger northern fireplace, even though bricks were the predominant material used in fireplace construction. The dark stain of a builders' trench, about one foot (thirty centimeters) wide, completely outlines the perimeter of the cellar (figs. 2.8 and 2.9), but no

FIG. 2.8. A closeup of the builders' trench in the cellar floor that completely outlines the sutling house. The scale board is marked in 10-cm increments and points north.

FIG. 2.9. The southeast corner of the sutling house in the summer of 2007. This is a view of the builders' trenches in the cellar floor, plus the partially exposed surface of the southern staircase. The lower courses of the staircase were removed in 2001–2002 before it was realized that the burned boards were part of a feature.

stones or bricks held up the walls: It was an earth-fast building, with all of the weight carried on posts that were set into the builders' trench. Plank walls no doubt held back the surrounding sand and kept the cellar from filling in. The builders' trench contains an ample supply of artifacts, including many pieces of lead buckshot, fish bones, occasional bricks, and even a complete wine bottle (fig. 2.10). Along the north wall of the cellar we found the burned bases of vertical posts that had been preserved in situ, rising out of the builder's trench, and these still support the remains of horizontal boards. We found the same type of construction on the other sides of the building—verticals rising out of a builder's trench—but not as well preserved as on the north. Window glass was found throughout the cellar, suggesting that the structure must have had windows, but nowhere was window glass so frequent as to suggest that it was a commonly sold commodity.

The most imposing structural feature that has survived within the ruins of the sutling house is a burned staircase, located at the northeast corner of the house and running from the cellar floor to the outside of the building (where bulkhead doors probably provided entry into the cellar) (fig. 2.11). In 2002 we had found door hinges lying on the cellar floor, but we did not discover until 2006 that the lower door—long since burned away—had

FIG. 2.10. A complete wine bottle, newly exposed in the builders' trench of the sutling house (facing south). The cork is gone, but the original wire that once anchored the cork still encircles the neck of the bottle. This is the only complete wine bottle we have discovered in eighteen years of digging in Fort Edward.

opened north and upward to a complete staircase positioned almost entirely outside the building. Steps, stringers, and risers had all been preserved by the burning, and we drew these in 2006 (figs. 2.12, 2.13, and 2.14). Fanning outward from where the upper, outside door had been, we found dozens of clothing fasteners (hooks and eyes) and large numbers of coins, suggesting soldiers waiting with their money in hand as their wine bottles were filled from kegs in the cellar. (Later, in 1759, were their bottles filled with freshly brewed spruce beer?) Artifacts were scattered along the surface of

FIG. 2.11. The northeast corner of the cellar, showing the burned staircase shortly after it was first exposed in the summer of 2006. Period artifacts (small bone fragments, tobacco pipes, coins, a knife, a key, ice creepers, and a butt plate) were scattered along the surface of the staircase and also just underneath the steps. Both scales are marked in 10-cm increments, and the scale arrow points north.

FIG. 2.12. Drawing to scale the elevation (profile) of the northern staircase (summer 2006). All measurements were taken downward from a level stringline and tape.

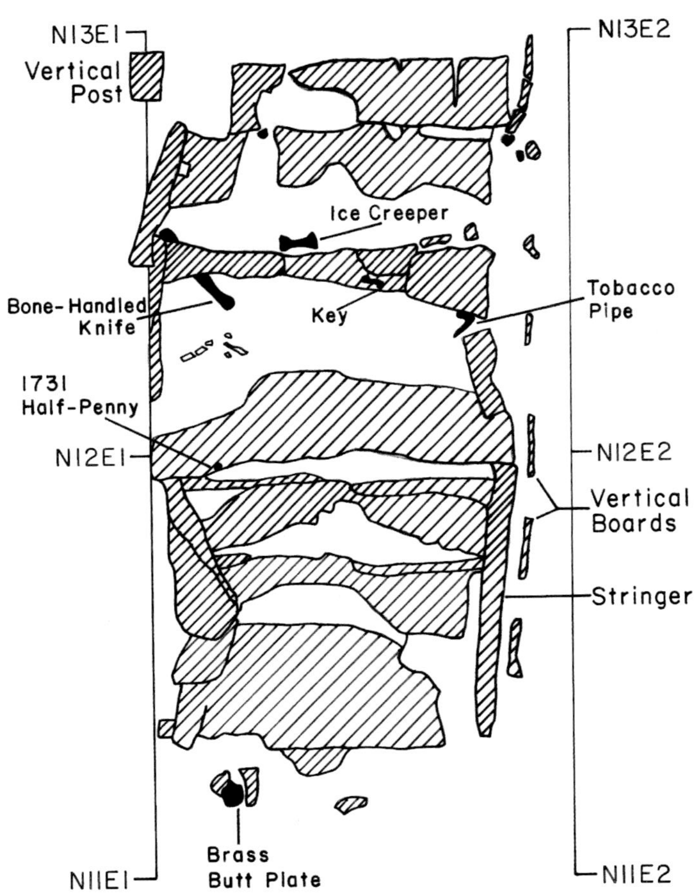

FIG. 2.13. A plan view of the northern staircase. The vertical post at the northwest corner appears to have anchored one side of the door frame at the top of the staircase.

(and underneath) the boards of the staircase, including the brass buttplate from a Brown Bess musket, a complete bone-handled table knife, and two ice creepers.

While this well-built staircase was probably the primary route whereby supplies were carried into and out of storage in the cellar, a second burned staircase was discovered in 2007 at the southeast corner of the cellar (figs. 2.9 and 2.15). This staircase was relatively crude, and the lowermost steps were missing, having been removed, unknowingly, by our own excavations in 2001 and 2002. Close to the southern staircase, lying on the cellar floor, we have found several thousand fragments of wine bottles, suggesting that this secondary entrance and staircase was used as the shortest route to wine and other spirits stored in the southern end of the building.

At several points along the west side of the cellar, we found iron barrel hoops, all that was left of barrels that had once stood on the cellar floor. On the east side of the cellar, we exposed a dense cluster of unused tobacco

FIG. 2.14. The elevation drawn of the northern staircase (see fig. 2.12). The upper and middle sections of the staircase were relatively intact, but only charcoal stains survived from the lower courses, where the staircase met the cellar floor.

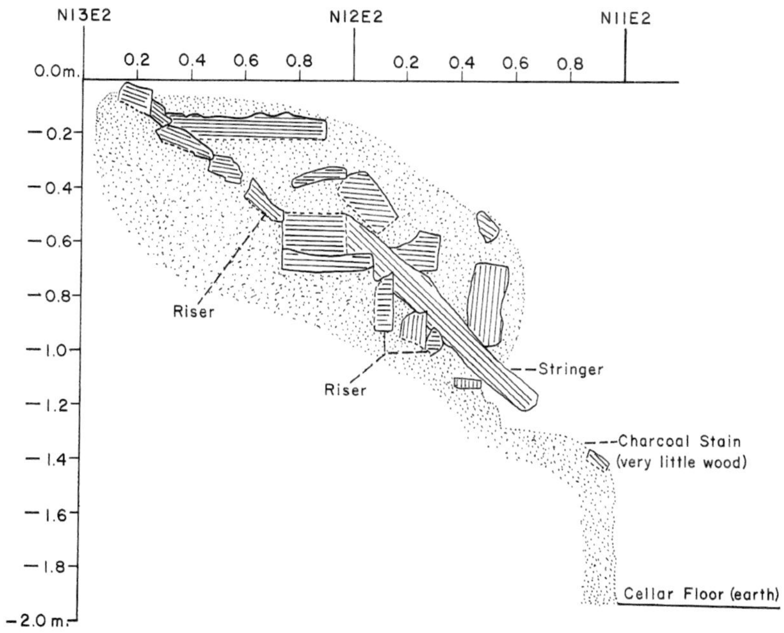

pipes, probably the contents of a keg or other container that held hundreds of pipes, a keg that flattened and broke when the building burned and collapsed. Most of these were RT (Robert Tippet) pipes, and a few thousand stem and bowl fragments are slowly being matched and glued together (see fig. 1.4).

Of the various finds on the cellar floor, coins represented one of the most diagnostic assemblages, and we found sixteen Spanish silver cobs, eight Spanish milled or "pillar" coins, and three Spanish one-bit pieces of eight (at least two of which were minted in Mexico City); thirty-eight British half-pence and four farthings; and even a French liard dating to 1695. But nothing prepared us for the discovery in 2006 of an Oak Tree Shilling, a Massachusetts colonial coin dated 1652 but actively in use over at least a thirty-year period, and sometimes in use even into the eighteenth century. It may have been nearly one hundred years old at the time it entered the deposits in the sutling house, and close to the rim it had been drilled with a small hole for hanging.

Other finds in the cellar included two complete Brown Bess bayonets and the socket from a third. One of these was found in the northern fireplace collapse and had been beautifully preserved, without rust, by the final conflagration. The other bayonets did not fare as well. A high water table has existed throughout the cellar down to the present day, and this has caused severe rusting of many ferrous artifacts, including the complete blade from a spade that was lying on the cellar floor just east of the northern

FIG. 2.15. A closeup of the crude staircase at the southeast corner of the sutling house (summer 2007). Three steps have survived, and the wood on the right (south) appears to be part of a side wall for the staircase.

FIG. 2.16. A pewter plate resting on the cellar floor of the sutling house (center of picture), surrounded by burned timbers and joists (facing west). Part of the northern, first-floor fireplace, collapsed into the cellar, appears on the left.

fireplace collapse. The stains from pewter buttons were also observed in several places, disintegrated beyond recovery.

Unquestionably our rarest finds were two complete ten-inch-diameter pewter plates that we discovered on the cellar floor toward the northern end of the house. The wet, acidic soil had removed almost all of the metal content from one plate, but three musket balls still rested on it, and seven other musket balls lay in the soil around it (fig. 2.16). When the plate was soaked with polyethylene glycol in an effort to consolidate it before removal from the ground, the pewter proved to be more stain than metal, and the wax ran right through it. The second pewter plate rested upside down about 5.4

meters to the southwest and was essentially complete. While oxidation had degraded its surface, the metal was solid, and it is easy to imagine soldiers or officers dining off pewter plates as they sat in the tavern.

Elsewhere on the cellar floor, we found two small delft ointment jars, both complete, by the northern staircase. There were many sherds from blue and white delft bowls and plates, and finds included the corroded side plate and screws from a Brown Bess musket. Fragments of bone-handled knives and forks lay everywhere, and even the small pits and postholes dug long ago into the cellar's earthen floor contained fragments of tobacco pipes. An unusual find was a large mass of lime in the center of the cellar floor, probably intended to be used in making mortar (fig. 2.17). One category of artifact we did *not* find, however, was fireplace furniture. There was no evidence for tongs, andirons, spits, etc., and there seems little doubt that some salvaging of the house's contents *must* have occurred either before or after the fire.

Perhaps the only truly unique find in the cellar was a glass bottle seal, the only bottle seal that we have found in eighteen years of excavations in Fort Edward. As yet unidentified, the family coat of arms has a rampant hound on one side and a guardant hound on the other. We also found fragments (usually bases) of glass medicine bottles and vials, bone combs, two padlocks and several keys, a variety of musket parts, many buckles, and much, much more.

At the start of our research, there were no comparative data with which to predict what we might find inside a mid-eighteenth-century sutling house. Now, eight years later, we have ample evidence that alcohol and tobacco

FIG. 2.17. A mass of lime discovered in the cellar floor of the sutling house. This was probably used in making mortar or plaster. The scale arrow points north.

FIG. 2.18. An overview of the sutling house excavation in the summer of 2007 (facing north). Both the central and southern parts of the house were still undergoing excavation at that time.

were the most popular commodities to be dispensed from what was probably the main sutling house in Fort Edward, but we have also found evidence for personal and clothing-related goods, and strong evidence for a tavern function. And everywhere there were coins, evidence of soldiers who were eager to bring their money to this establishment to buy merchandise or a meal. Our sutling house was a secure, reasonably well-built structure, more permanent than any of the huts and tents we have excavated at local military camps over the past eighteen years. Only the barracks buildings whose foundations we have exposed inside Fort Edward, Fort William Henry, and on Rogers Island were as substantial. This sutling house had a full cellar; massive brick fireplaces; a well-defined builder's trench; more than three thousand fragments of window glass; a substantial staircase that provided access to the cellar; a secondary staircase and cellar entrance; and several pairs of strap hinges that suggest where doors had formerly been located.

We do not have an exact date for the final fire or for when "Mr. Best" (or his successors) abandoned the sutling house, although the very end of 1759 seems likely, given the total evacuation of Fort Edward at that time. The quality of its construction—especially with two sizeable fireplaces on the main floor—is exceptionally good for a building that probably lasted for two years or less (fig. 2.18). A strong argument can be made that our sutling house suggests relative wealth and permanence, with a quantity and quality of artifacts that go well beyond any of the military camp sites where we have excavated in the past. After digging a point of supply *and* the points of consumption in Fort Edward, it is clear that the merchants in this house had good things to sell, and the soldiers were no doubt pleased to have goods from "home" that they could purchase here. This may well have been the most popular destination within the vast Fort Edward encampment of the 1750s. Two hundred and fifty years later, archeology is helping to define the layout and contents of a prosperous place of business, and Mr. Best's house has proven to be one of the most informative archeological sites ever discovered in Fort Edward or Lake George.

"*ye Cannon Fire Briskly at ye Lake and also ye Small arms*"
—Jabez Fitch, Jr.
(August 3, 1757)

3

Weaponry and Ammunition

General Overview

THE LONG LAND PATTERN of British flintlock musket, today better known as the "Brown Bess," was the principal firearm of the British Army throughout the French and Indian War, and its derivatives were still in use until the 1830s, when it was finally replaced by the percussion cap musket. It is extremely rare for archeology to recover intact muskets, swords, cannons, or other major pieces of weaponry from any terrestrial excavation site, although relatively complete weaponry has sometimes been found underwater in Lake George and Lake Champlain (Starbuck 1999b:chapter 8). The closest we have come to discovering intact weaponry on land digs in Lake George or Fort Edward is a complete musket barrel that we recovered from the bottom of a hut at the Lake George Battlefield Park (fig. 3.1). Only

FIG. 3.1. A barrel from a Brown Bess musket found *in situ* in 2001 inside a hut foundation at the Lake George Battlefield Park. This is the only complete musket barrel found during any of our excavations in Lake George or Fort Edward. Both scales are marked in 10-cm increments, and the scale arrow points north.

fragments of barrels have been found elsewhere, sometimes reflecting soldiers deliberately shortening their musket barrels.

Much more common at the New York sites are the gunflints and musket balls that archeologists have found in abundance at virtually every eighteenth-century military site (Hamilton and Emery 1988; Sivilich 1996). No doubt a majority of these flints and balls (typically measuring between 66 and 69 caliber) were used in the Brown Bess. The New York sites contain little evidence for balls less than 60 caliber (representing rifles) or for balls between 60 and 66 caliber (which would have been used in the French Charleville musket). Much less common at these sites are musket parts and bayonets, suggesting that soldiers guarded their weapons closely, and that parts were thrown away only when they were broken beyond repair. Only during the very extensive excavations at Fort Michilimackinac (Hamilton 1976), Fort Ligonier (Grimm 1970), and Fort Stanwix (Hanson and Hsu 1975) did archeologists recover relatively large numbers of parts from weapons.

No inventory or quantification exists for all of the weapons, musket balls, and gunflints removed from Rogers Island by Earl Stott and the Rogers Island Historical Association, whose finds included cannonballs, four complete Brown Bess bayonets, and many chewed musket balls (Rogers Island Historical Association 1986:26–27). Stott often claimed that chewed musket balls meant that soldiers bit down on these while being lashed at the whipping post. While that may sometimes have been true, other interpretations have included biting on the musket balls during surgery or amputation, sucking on musket balls to promote salivation, chewing on the balls to make them spin while in flight, and—the most recent interpretation—that some of the tooth marks were left by animals, especially pigs and squirrels. This last interpretation is the result of innovative research conducted by Daniel Sivilich and Henry Miller, who—among other experiments—chewed on fresh, 69 caliber musket balls to see what patterns are actually left by human tooth marks (Sivilich, personal communication, October 25, 2008).

Unquestionably the most remarkable find made on Rogers Island by the Rogers Island Historical Association was an intact pocket sundial and compass (fig. 3.2):

> The inside revealed a combination sundial and compass. The cover contained a printed compass rose on a paper disc with principal and minor compass points. The base contained the sundial mounted over a glass with the magnetic compass below it. The "style" on the sundial was collapsible and the hours were neatly engraved on the brass dial ring in Roman numerals. (Rogers Island Historical Association 1986:27)

FIG. 3.2. The brass pocket sundial and compass that Earl Stott discovered in 1965 in some fireplace bricks in a hut site on Rogers Island. Now on display in the Fort Ticonderoga Museum, it is one of the finest examples of an early compass to be found archeologically (1¾ inches in diameter). The top has a screw-on thread, and "the British Museum revealed that this sundial-compass was made in Germany between 1730 and 1740 and was exported to England for use here" (Rogers Island Historical Association 1986: 27). *Courtesy of Winston Adler.*

FIG. 3.3. Left: A brass compass case (three inches in diameter), discovered in Fort Edward (the McDougall Collection). Right: A modern brass reproduction of the compass in fig. 3.2.

This superb brass compass has subsequently been reproduced and marketed by Son Manufacturing Company (fig. 3.3, right).

Our own more recent excavations on Rogers Island (1991–1998) recovered an excellent collection of weapon parts and ammunition, including four bayonet fragments, three hundred and twenty-two musket balls, five hundred and thirty-one pieces of buckshot and birdshot, two hundred and sixty-seven British and French gunflints (including fragments), four scab-

FIG. 3.4. Weapon-related artifacts from a single hut (Site 19) on Rogers Island. These include British gunflints, lead shot and sprue (center), musket balls, and a scabbard holder (top).

FIG. 3.5. A cluster of forty-five musket balls discovered in 1992 underneath the dirt floor of Dwelling 1 (a tent) on Rogers Island.

bard holders (frogs), and thirteen musket parts of various types (figs. 3.4 and 3.5) (Starbuck 2004:80, 83). Given the proportion of Rogers Island that was occupied during the French and Indian War (at least twenty acres) and the modest extent of our own excavations, these artifacts are undoubtedly a very small sample of the armaments that still remain on the island.

The centerpiece of the great military camps in Fort Edward was, of course, the 1755 fort itself, and the McDougall Collection, assembled from

FIG. 3.6. An English iron halberd discovered in Fort Edward (nine inches tall and seven inches wide). By the eighteenth century, halberds primarily functioned as a symbol of authority, but these are rarely found on archeological sites. *From the McDougall Collection*

FIG. 3.7. Bayonets from Fort Edward. The upper two bayonets were made for the British Brown Bess musket, and a plug bayonet appears at the bottom (top to bottom: 18⅝ inches long, 11½ inches long, and 17¼ inches long). *From the McDougall Collection*

private digging on Moon Street, best reflects the weaponry surviving within the fort. This exceptional collection includes the complete head from a halberd (fig. 3.6), a brass compass case (fig. 3.3, left), three bayonets (fig. 3.7), thirty-six pieces of cast iron grapeshot, several British gunflints (fig. 3.8), and an assortment of weapon parts that include Brown Bess side plates, ramrod tips, a ramrod pipe, Brown Bess trigger guards, a sling swivel, and a musket cock (fig. 3.9). The McDougall Collection also contains a

FIG. 3.8. British gunflints from Fort Edward. *From the McDougall Collection*

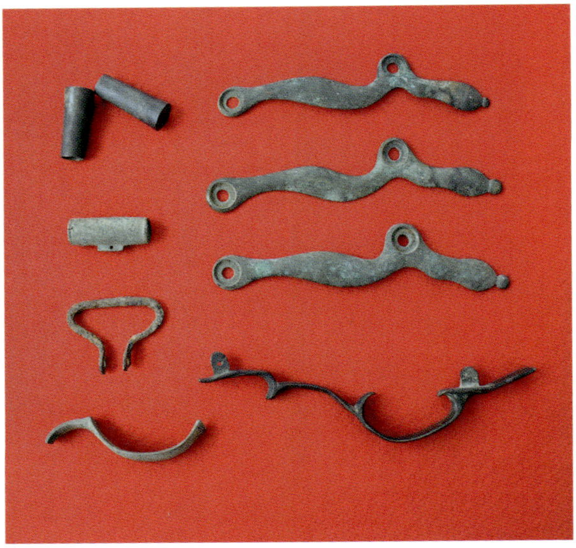

FIG. 3.9. Weaponry from Fort Edward. Left, top to bottom: two brass tips for wood ramrods (each is 1½ inches long); ramrod pipe (1¹¹⁄₁₆ inches long); brass sling swivel (2⅟₁₆ inches by 1½ inches); brass trigger guard fragment (3⅜ inches long). Right, top to bottom: three Brown Bess brass side plates (5¹³⁄₁₆ inches long, 6¼ inches long, 6¼ inches long); Brown Bess brass trigger guard (7 inches long). *From the McDougall Collection.*

FIG. 3.10. The lead ingot at the top (4½ by 1 by 2 inches) and the three chewed musket balls (lower right) are from Fort Edward (the McDougall Collection). The two smaller lead ingots on the lower left are both from the sutling house in Fort Edward (left: 1⅝ by 1⅛ by 1¼ inches; right: 1½ by 1⅝ by 1 inches).

FIG. 3.11. An iron halberd on display in the Fort William Henry Museum (from the 1950s excavation).

very large ingot that would have provided lead for making musket balls (fig. 3.10, top).

Within the village of Lake George, the scale of the 1950s excavation at Fort William Henry ensured that large quantities of weapons and ammunition were recovered from that site, including a halberd (fig. 3.11), numer-

FIG. 3.12. Bayonets from the 1950s excavation at Fort William Henry, now on display in the Fort William Henry Museum.

FIG. 3.13. Some of the mortar shell fragments excavated from Fort William Henry in the 1950s. These have been selected from a collection of one hundred and sixty-one fragments, and they vary in breadth from five to seven inches.

FIG. 3.14. Lead buckshot excavated from Fort William Henry in the 1950s. These have been selected from a total of four hundred and thirty-nine balls of various calibers.

ous bayonets (fig. 3.12), and very large quantities of mortar shell fragments, buckshot, and gunflints (figs. 3.13, 3.14, and 3.15). Some of the more impressive of these artifacts are currently on display in the Fort William Henry Museum, with the remaining pieces in storage at the fort.

The more recent excavations at Fort William Henry by Adirondack Com-

FIG. 3.15. Gunflints excavated in the 1950s at Fort William Henry. Most of these are British, and many have been discolored by fire.

FIG. 3.16. Representative gunflints excavated from the dump east of Fort William Henry in the 1990s (nearly all are British).

munity College between 1997 and 2000 recovered just two bayonet fragments, but finds included two hundred and fifty-nine musket balls, fourteen pieces of lead shot, one hundred and ninety-five British and French gunflints (including fragments) (fig. 3.16), thirteen pieces of grapeshot, eighteen pieces of canister shot, eighteen pieces of mortar shells, two "worms" (for extracting loads that had not fired), and very low numbers of musket parts (see Starbuck 2002b:appendix 2). The violent nature of the fort's demise, coupled with the many years of digging, resulted in an excellent collection of material from that fort.

FIG. 3.17. A British gunflint still set into its lead gunflint patch, found during amateur metal detecting in the Birch Avenue area west of Route 9 in Lake George.

FIG. 3.18. A complete bayonet *in situ* in 2001 within a test pit at the Lake George Battlefield Park. The scale arrow is marked in 10-cm increments and points north.

Other sites in Lake George have not seen the same level of digging, but the collection that was recovered by amateur metal detecting in the Birch Avenue area (on the west side of Route 9) contained two cannonballs, twenty-nine musket balls (six of which had been chewed), three ramrod pipes, and one gunflint still set into its lead patch (fig. 3.17). Elsewhere, archeology conducted by Adirondack Community College at the Lake George Battlefield Park in 2000–2001 recovered a complete Brown Bess bayonet (fig. 3.18), the intact musket barrel already mentioned (fig. 3.1), a single cannonball, musket balls, gunflints, grapeshot, a frizzen, and a ramrod

FIG. 3.20. A brass compass discovered in 2001 at the Lake George Battlefield Park. The Roman numeral "XXIX" is scratched into the case, indicating this was the property of the British 29th Regiment of Foot (1¾ inches in diameter).

FIG. 3.19. Weaponry from the Lake George Battlefield Park. Left: ramrod pipe (1½ inches long). Right: frizzen (2⅜ inches tall). Bottom: musket lock main spring (3½ inches long).

pipe (fig. 3.19). While all of these finds are significant, none quite compares with a remarkable brass compass discovered within the park in 2001, complete with the Roman numerals "XXIX" etched into the case (fig. 3.20). Based upon the historically documented movements of the British 29th Regiment of Foot, this clearly was left there during the Revolutionary War period.

The Sutling House

The sutling house in Fort Edward does not appear to have been a significant source of weaponry to the British Army, nor would that have been necessary. New recruits were issued a "stand of arms," and "The box with frog and belt were part of this stand, in addition to the musket with its sling, bayonet, and scabbard" (Troiani 1998:4). Still, the remains of the sutling house did contain one hundred and five musket balls and one hundred and fifty-three pieces of lead shot (fig. 3.21), and forty-one British and French gunflints (twice as many British flints as French—see examples in fig. 3.22), as well as two musket cocks, two ramrod pipes, two wrist escutcheon plates, two scabbard tips, a butt plate, a scabbard holder (frog), and several small lead ingots, probably used for casting musket balls and shot (figs. 3.23, 3.24, and 3.10, bottom left). We even found the complete brass lockplate and associated screws from a musket on the cellar floor of the sutling house. We also discovered two complete bayonets and fragments of three others (fig. 3.25). Virtually all the musket parts and fragments of weaponry found in the sutling house were designed for the British Brown Bess musket (see appendix).

FIG. 3.21. Lead musket balls and shot (various calibers) from the sutling house in Fort Edward. Some of the balls have not yet been filed down to make them suitable for firing.

FIG. 3.22. Examples of gunflints found in the Fort Edward sutling house. The top two rows are British gunflints, and the bottom row is French.

FIG. 3.23. Weaponry discovered in the Fort Edward sutling house. Left: Brown Bess brass butt plate (4¾ inches long); Top center: cock (hammer) with gunflint (3½ inches tall). Top right: cock (3¼ inches tall). Middle: ramrod pipes (left: 1½ inches long; right: ⅞ inch long); Bottom: brass scabbard holder (frog) with a small amount of leather still attached (2½ inches long).

FIG. 3.24. A brass wrist escutcheon plate from a Brown Bess musket, found in the sutling house in Fort Edward (2¼ inches long).

FIG. 3.25. Two Brown Bess bayonets discovered in the cellar hole of the sutling house in Fort Edward (both are 21½ inches long). The upper bayonet rested within the collapsed rubble from the northern fireplace, where it was discovered together with a complete bone-handled table knife and a complete tobacco pipe.

FIG. 3.26. Lead sows from the sutling house in Fort Edward. Each has three to eight nipples, indicating where musket balls were detached from the sprue.

Interestingly enough, there were no chewed musket balls inside the sutling house, and only one chewed piece of lead shot, unlike encampment areas, where chewed balls have appeared in some numbers. However, lead "sows" were common (fig. 3.26), revealing that musket balls and shot were being made in or near the sutling house.

"At Night We Drinked three Quarts of Cherry Rhum"
—Jabez Fitch, Jr.
(October 18, 1757)

4

Food and Foodways, Cutlery, Pottery, and Glass

General Overview

SOLDIERS' AND OFFICERS' diaries from the eighteenth century make constant references to food and meals, and no doubt food was a favorite discussion topic every day at the forts and encampments! For example, Jabez Fitch, Jr., while based in Fort Edward in 1757, mentioned "we were Vary Hungry Provision Vary Short about Noon we Cookd Some Rice without Sweetning Butter or Salt But it Tasted Vary Good" (Fitch, Jr. 1986:2) and "at Night Chappel & I Bought Som Fresh Fish & Invited ye Capt: to Supper with Us" (p. 21). Fitch went on to recount, "At Night We Drinked Three Quarts of Cherry Rhum at our tent" (p. 29). Also, "In ye Morning we Eat Som Cake & Cheese & Drinkd Som Sider" (p. 32) and "This Day I Dined At Capt: Durkes on Som Rosted Venson & Pickeld Oysters" (p. 38).

Beverages of the period would have included coffee, tea, chocolate, cider, rum, brandy, and wine, and soldiers and officers might have dined on beef, pork, fish, mutton, venison, shellfish, bread, cheese, and a variety of vegetables, both fresh and dried. A cooking kit of the French and Indian War might have included cast iron pots and camp kettles, copper skillets, frying pans, skewers, and baking pots. The setting for the cooking could have been as diverse as a free-standing oven, a fireplace inside a barracks, or a spit over an open fire (fig. 4.1). The actual consumption was from an extremely diverse assortment of earthenwares and stonewares, no doubt including bottles, plates, or whatever else had not yet broken after months in the field. Officers had tea sets, helping to reinforce their higher status, but "fine dining" does not come to mind when most of these wares are examined.

Contemporary journals shed much light on food and foodways, but they

FIG. 4.1. Steven Collyer, a modern reenactor, demonstrates some of the equipment necessary for fine eighteenth-century dining!

rarely give any quantitative sense of what was being consumed. Archeological remains, on the other hand, actually do provide very direct evidence. Animal bones are abundant and are a reasonably good indicator of what went into the meat portion of the diet (fig. 4.2). We have discovered thousands of butchered animal bones and teeth at every military camp, and occasionally even horns. Cow and pig predominate, but they are accompanied by small quantities of deer and fish. Salted beef and pork leave no bones behind, but the bones we found suggest that there was ample fresh meat, both domesticated and wild. Plant remains do not survive as well archeologically, unless charred, so these are harder to quantify.

All of the military sites we studied in Fort Edward and Lake George contain cutlery and vessels that were used in the preparation and consumption of food, and these include modest numbers of bone-handled table knives, bone-handled forks, and pewter spoons, large numbers of dark-green wine bottle fragments, a smattering of wine glass fragments, and fairly homogeneous assemblages of ceramics. The plates, cups, saucers, and bowls at every site are mostly manufactured of delft (tin-glazed earthenware) and white salt-glazed stoneware. (Tin-glazed earthenware also accounted for the largest number of sherds at Fort Michilimackinac—see Miller and Stone 1970.) Still, these sites also have smaller numbers of sherds of unrefined stoneware and porcelain, and there are just a few sherds of buff-bodied, slip-decorated earthenware (which was quite out-of-date by the 1750s). The unrefined stoneware appears in the form of jugs and crocks—storage vessels—whereas the cups and saucers clearly derive from tea sets. A significant proportion of the white salt-glazed stoneware was decorated with "scratch blue," with cobalt filling in the patterns of incised lines. Fragments of wine glasses tend to be rare at every site, suggesting that we may have located very few officers' huts or dumps. Interestingly enough, cookingware is the rarest part of these food-related assemblages: Pot and kettle fragments and even andirons and spits are almost nonexistent in the archeological record at these sites.

Digs conducted by the Rogers Island Historical Association discovered significant numbers of sherds of delft and unrefined stoneware on Rogers Island, along with wine bottles and canteen fragments, but only the recent work (1991–1998) by Adirondack Community College on Rogers Island provides any quantification (Starbuck 2004:appendix I). Excavations in a wide variety of contexts on the island recovered 1,347 sherds of delft, four hundred and twenty-two sherds of white salt-glazed stoneware, three hundred and eighty sherds of redware, two hundred and forty-nine sherds of porcelain, and one hundred and fifty-six sherds of unrefined stoneware (figs. 4.3 and 4.4). Pottery and porcelain were accompanied by 2,285 wine bottle fragments, many canteen fragments (figs. 4.5 and 4.6), thirteen knives, five forks, and fragments of twenty-two pewter spoons (figs. 4.7 and 4.8). Wine glasses were extremely rare, as were fragments of pots or kettles. Glass medicine bottles were well represented, although most of

FIG. 4.2. A dump for food remains that lies about fifty feet northeast of the cellar hole of the sutling house in Fort Edward. Butchered animal bones are scattered throughout the earth here, accompanied by a two-tined fork. The scale arrow points north.

FIG. 4.3. Representative sherds of unrefined stoneware (top left and bottom left), redware (top right), delft (center), white salt-glazed stoneware with scratch blue decoration (center right), and Chinese export porcelain (bottom right), all found at campsites on Rogers Island.

FIG. 4.4. The rim and side of a chamber pot of unrefined stoneware excavated from a soldiers' dump on Rogers Island (the rim is 7⅝ inches in diameter).

FIG. 4.7. (opposite) Knives and knife fragments found on Rogers Island. The bone knife handle at the top was found in an officers' dump; the second and fourth knives down are complete folding knives; and the knife fragment that is the third down is the blade from a table knife. "They would have [had] personal knives of many different varieties. Some could have even been folding, pocket style knives. I do not think many of them would have been very large. Large knives might look impressive, but usually are not as practical as smaller ones" (Tim Todish, personal communication, February 9, 2008).

FIG. 4.5. A canteen discovered by a collector in a backhoe trench on Rogers Island in 1988, prior to conservation (10½ inches long).

FIG. 4.6. The same canteen that appears in fig. 4.5, after conservation by Nancy Demetteneyre, New York State Office of Parks, Recreation and Historic Preservation.

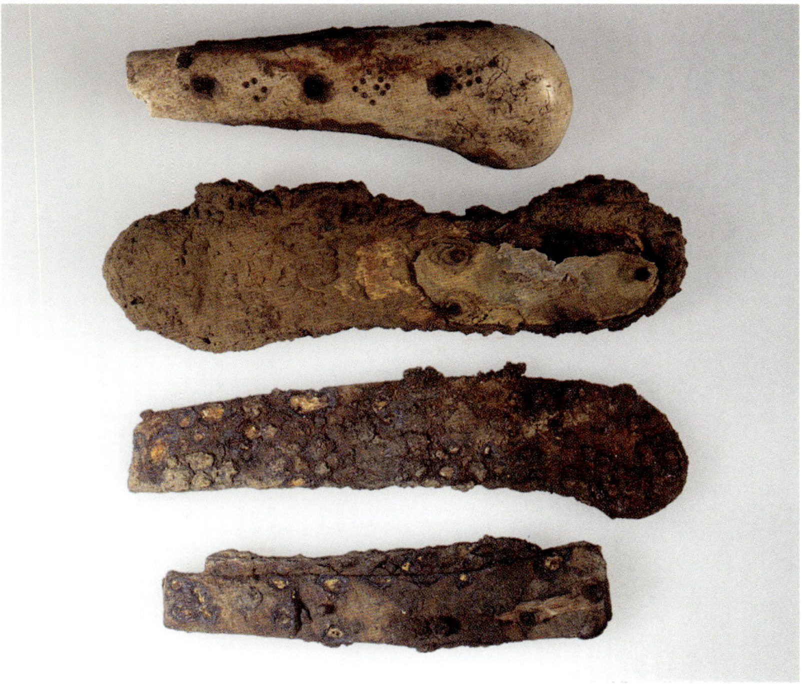

FIG. 4.8. A badly deteriorated pewter spoon discovered on the floor of Dwelling 5 (an officers' house) on Rogers Island.

FIG. 4.9. A medicine bottle discovered inside the remains of Dwelling 5 (an officers' house) on Rogers Island (3¼ inches long). This is the most common form of medicine bottle in both Fort Edward and Lake George, but it is rare to find a bottle this intact.

these were extremely fragmentary (the only intact example from our work on Rogers Island appears in fig. 4.9).

Recovered from the fort in Fort Edward, within the McDougall Collection, are a well-preserved copper skillet, a pewter cup, and a total of five two-tined forks (fig. 4.10), but there is little pottery or glass in the collection. Still, this small but rich assemblage suggests that future excavations within barracks areas of the fort might provide an excellent opportunity to expose fireplaces and cooking and dining areas.

Turning to the village of Lake George, the Fort William Henry Museum retains only very small quantities of pottery and porcelain from the 1950s' excavation, but the 1990s' dig at the fort by Adirondack Community College recovered considerable pottery, glassware, and butchered animal bones (Starbuck 2002b). In fact, the dump that was excavated just east of the fort (Site 5) chiefly contained food-related debris (more than fifteen thousand butchered bones and much pottery and glass). Altogether, from various contexts within the fort, we excavated four hundred and twenty-four sherds of white salt-glazed stoneware, three hundred and fifty-nine sherds of delft, two hundred and sixty-one sherds of redware, more than one thousand fragments of wine bottles, six knives, two forks, and five spoons (figs. 4.11 and 4.12).

FIG. 4.10. A copper skillet, pewter cup, and two bone-handled iron forks from Fort Edward (the McDougall Collection), and a copper kettle rim with lug (bottom) excavated from the northeast corner of the sutling house in Fort Edward. (The copper skillet measures 11¾ by 10$^{11}/_{16}$ inches; the copper kettle fragment is 8 inches long; the pewter cup is 2 inches tall and 2 inches in diameter; and the forks are both 6½ inches long.)

FIG. 4.11. Representative sherds recovered during the 1990s' excavations at Fort William Henry, consisting of delft (top left, top center, and left center), Chinese export porcelain (bottom left), white salt-glazed stoneware with scratch blue decoration (bottom right), and buff-bodied, slip-decorated earthenware (top right).

FIG. 4.12. A small brass spoon (top: 2¼ inches long) and the bone inlay from a knife handle (bottom: ¾ inch long), both from the 1990s' excavation of the West Barracks at Fort William Henry.

FIG. 4.13. Pewter spoons (and fragments) discovered by a collector with a metal detector at military camps west of Route 9 at the south end of the village of Lake George.

The amateur metal detecting in the Birch Avenue section of Lake George located fragments of four pewter spoons (fig. 4.13), as well as a complete bone-handled table knife. The 2000–2001 excavations at the Lake George Battlefield Park recovered numerous wine bottles, a two-tined fork with a bone handle, several knife blades, and the bowl from a small brass spoon, but the quantities of food-related artifacts were very low. However, two sherds from a plate of white salt-glazed stoneware with dot, diaper, and basket pattern were excavated from the remains of a barracks in the park (fig. 4.14), and this is an exceptionally rare decorative pattern at any of the military camps.

FIG. 4.14. Sherds from a white salt-glazed stoneware plate with dot, diaper, and basket pattern, found in a barracks foundation at the Lake George Battlefield Park.

FIG. 4.15. Fish bones found chiefly within the north wall builders' trench of the Fort Edward sutling house. All of these are vertebrae, except for the top left bone, which is a preoperculum.

The Sutling House

Artifacts recovered from the cellar hole of the sutling house in Fort Edward, when combined with artifacts from its associated dumps, included a total of 4,090 bones and bone fragments, as well as one hundred and seventy-eight teeth (see appendix). Most of these derive from cow and pig, although we did discover significant numbers of sheep bones, bird bones and fish bones (fig. 4.15). This represents somewhat more diversity in species than we have typically recovered from the sites of huts, tents, and barracks. Several sheep mandibles were also found at the sutling house, which raises the provocative question of whether soldiers went to the sutling house specifically to dine on foods that they could not obtain as part of their regular issue.

Dark-green wine bottles were the most plentiful category of artifact in the sutling house, and some 9,113 fragments were found, including one

FIG. 4.16. Examples of wine bottles from the sutling house in Fort Edward. The center bottle is complete, while the others are in the process of being mended. The bottle on the right is severely melted, probably from the fire that razed the sutling house.

FIG. 4.17. The seal from the shoulder of a wine bottle, found just outside the cellar hole of the sutling house in Fort Edward. An English viscount crown appears at the top of the seal, and hounds (one rampant and one guardant) appear on the two sides. *Rebekah Barrett, Personal Communication, 2009.*

complete bottle (fig. 4.16) and one bottle seal (fig. 4.17). These represented hundreds of bottles that were being stored in the cellar of the house, with a majority of the bottles located in the southern half of the building. Since spirits were typically stored in barrels and dispensed into bottles, it was somewhat unexpected to find this many bottles inside the building. It is also tempting to ask whether some of these might pertain to the spruce beer brewery, authorized by General Amherst, that was constructed at or near the site in 1759.

There were just ninety-four fragments of square-sided case bottles, occasional fragments of medicine bottles (fig. 4.18), and even the rim from a snuff bottle (fig. 4.19). However, the most distinctive aspect of this assemblage of glassware was the high proportion of glass tablewares, chiefly wine glasses, which were much more common in the sutling house than at any campsite, fort, or barracks that we have excavated (figs. 4.20 and 4.18, lower right). These were found throughout the cellar, although they were especially common in the northern half of the building, where tavern activities appear to have been concentrated. There were more than a thousand fragments of stemware altogether, including two stems with an "air-twist" pattern (the larger fragment appears in fig. 4.18, bottom right). One of the most diagnostic discoveries was a firing glass (fig. 4.18, bottom left), typified by the thick stem and heavy foot that enabled it to be hammered

FIG. 4.18. Fragments of medicine (apothecary) bottles (top row), a firing glass (bottom left: base diameter 2⅜ inches and 2⅝ inches tall), and a wine glass with air-twist stem (bottom right: fragment is 4⅛ inches long). All are from the sutling house in Fort Edward.

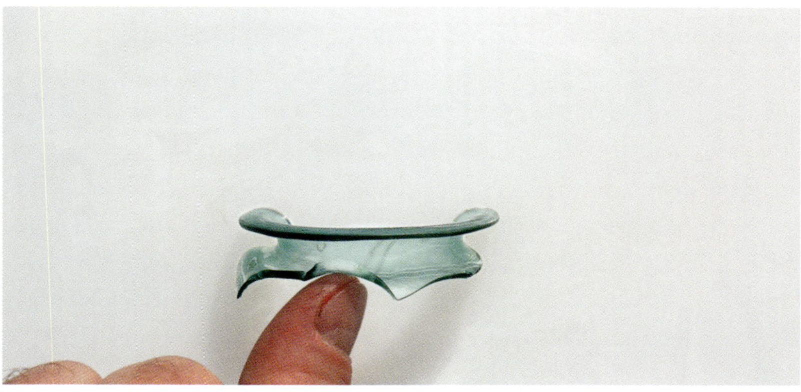

FIG. 4.19. The rim from a square snuff bottle found in the cellar of the sutling house in Fort Edward. Parchment or vellum would have been stretched over the top (and over the curled lip) and tied with a cord (2⅛ inches outside diameter).

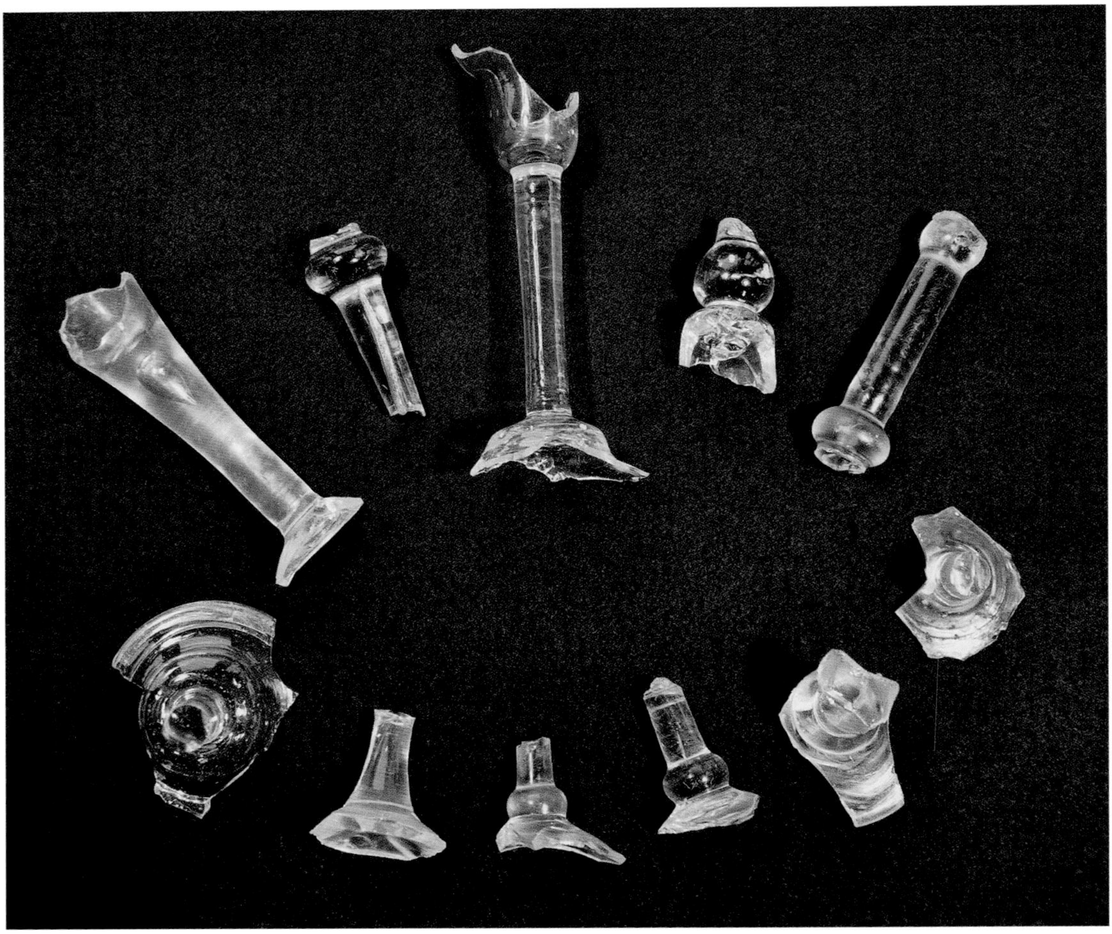

FIG. 4.20. Representative wine glass stems and bases found inside the Fort Edward sutling house. The relatively complete wine glass in top center has a pan topped bowl, plain pillar stem, and terraced foot (it is five inches tall).

down onto tabletops during toasts (Brown 1971:120–121; Jones and Smith 1985:52) (see the appendix).

Ceramic vessels in the sutling house were plentiful, represented by 2,936 sherds of delft, eight hundred and forty sherds of white salt-glazed stoneware, one hundred and forty-nine sherds of white salt-glazed with scratch blue decoration (figs. 4.21 and 4.22), and smaller quantities of redware, porcelain, and unrefined stoneware. Much of this assemblage appears to have been tavern ware, and delft was used for bowls (typically six to seven inches in diameter and three inches high), plates, tea cups, ointment jars (two were complete), and at least one charger (figs. 4.23, 4.24, and 4.25). White salt-glazed stoneware appeared principally as cups and saucers, although we discovered sherds from a single eight-inch-diameter white salt-glazed stoneware plate (undecorated) inside the builders' trench on the eastern side of the building (fig. 4.26, left), plus the lid from a teapot and a

FIG. 4.21. Representative cup, saucer, and bowl sherds of white salt-glazed stoneware with scratch blue decoration, all from the Fort Edward sutling house.

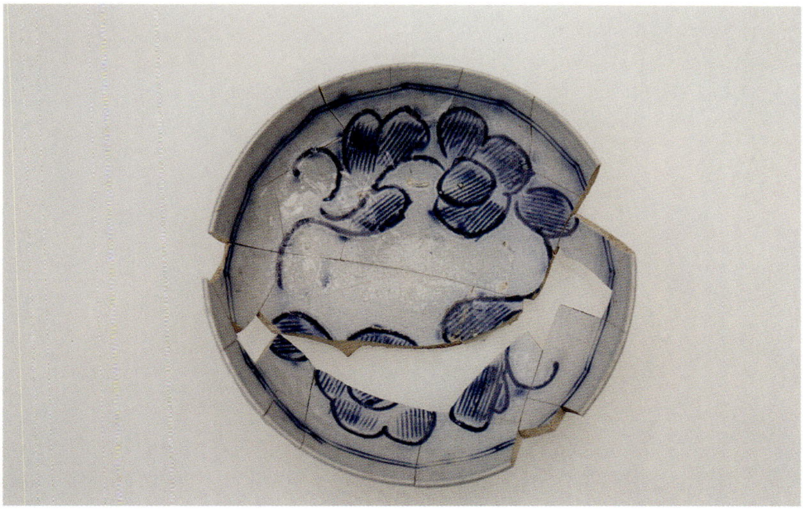

FIG. 4.22. A saucer of white salt-glazed stoneware with scratch blue decoration, found in the sutling house in Fort Edward (four inches in diameter).

FIG. 4.23. A six-inch-diameter English delft bowl found at the north end of the cellar in the Fort Edward sutling house (height is three inches).

FIG. 4.24. Sherds of English delft from the Fort Edward sutling house, all undergoing mending. These represent three bowls, a plate, and a platter.

FIG. 4.25. Two delft ointment jars discovered next to the northern staircase in the Fort Edward sutling house (each is 1⅜ inches tall and 2¹⁄₁₆ inches in diameter).

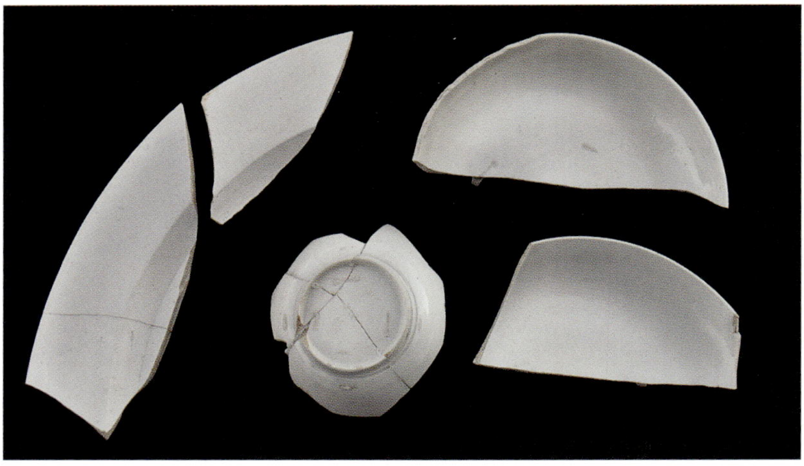

FIG. 4.26. White salt-glazed stoneware plate, cup, and saucer sherds, found in the sutling house in Fort Edward.

FIG. 4.27. Left: a teapot lid ($1^{11}/_{16}$ inches in diameter). Right: a plate rimsherd with "bead and reel" decoration. Both are white salt-glazed stoneware, and both were discovered in the cellar of the Fort Edward sutling house.

single rim sherd from a plate that had bead and reel decoration (fig. 4.27) (see the appendix).

Cutlery in the sutling house was also more common than in any encampment site, and we recovered fifteen forks or fork fragments, eighteen table knives or knife fragments, and seven bone handles that could have broken away from either forks or knives (figs. 4.28 and 4.29). Some of the bone handles were decorated, and others were not. The frequency of cutlery provides additional support for a "tavern" interpretation for the sutling

FIG. 4.28. Examples of cutlery discovered in the cellar of the Fort Edward sutling house, including two pewter spoon handles (upper right).

FIG. 4.29. Iron table knives with bone handles found in the "tavern area" at the north end of the sutling house in Fort Edward (top: 9½ inches long; bottom: 10¾ inches long). Both knives have a dorsal ridge partway along the blade, and the upper knife has a pistol-grip handle.

FIG. 4.30. A pewter dinner plate on the cellar floor of the sutling house in Fort Edward, discovered in 2006 with three musket balls resting on its surface (see fig. 2.16). This was 1.88 m below the modern ground surface, and very little metal has survived. When melted polyethylene glycol (PEG) was poured over its surface to consolidate the plate, the wax ran through the gray stain.

house, but spoons were curiously underrepresented: We recovered only two pewter spoon handles and no spoon bowls (fig. 4.28, upper right).

Our most exciting discovery within the sutling house was surely the two pewter plates that we recovered in 2006 and 2008, both resting on the cellar floor and with the collapsed rubble from the northern fireplace lying between them. Both plates measured ten inches in diameter—they were identical dinner plates—but the degree of preservation was very different. One plate survived only as a stain (fig. 4.30), while the other plate was largely intact (figs. 4.31 and 4.32). No pewter plates had previously been discovered at any of our other dig sites in Fort Edward or Lake George, and given the acidity of the soil, this level of preservation was really very special.

FIG. 4.31. A pewter dinner plate discovered in 2008 on the cellar floor of the sutling house in Fort Edward. The plate was upside down and 1.71 m below the modern ground surface. The metric rod is marked in 10-cm increments, and the scale arrow points north.

FIG. 4.32. The ten-inch-diameter pewter plate that appears in fig. 4.31, after preliminary cleaning.

While no clearly identifiable cooking vessels were located, the sutlers' site nevertheless contained a flattened rim fragment from a copper kettle (fig. 4.10, bottom), as well as a cast iron handle that appears to be from a cooking pan. These were accompanied by some ninety-five fragments of copper kettles, all too small to reveal their original shape(s).

The large quantities of ceramic and glass vessels and cutlery strongly reinforce our interpretation that a tavern functioned within the sutling house, and clearly a great many of the artifacts pertain to wining and dining. All things considered, this establishment would have been a great place for Jabez Fitch to "drink some Cherry Rhum," eat some venison and cheese, and discuss the progress of the war with his fellow soldiers!

"Got Some Tools"
—Jabez Fitch, Jr.
(June 2, 1757)

5

Tools and Equipment

General Overview

TOOLS OF MANY TYPES were essential at British military camps of the eighteenth century, including felling axes for hewing wood, belt axes (fig. 5.1), spades and shovels for digging trenches and creating earthworks, fascine knives for clearing brush, pike and pole tips and pole support rings, hoes, chisels, files, hammers, padlocks, keys, ice creepers (attached to the bottoms of shoes in the winter), and a great many more. For convenience, other categories of equipment are considered here as well, including ox shoes and horseshoes, stirrups, barrel hoops, tin buckets, and wagon wheel hardware.

FIG. 5.1. The discovery of a belt axe in the Fort Edward sutling house. Many of these were found by the Rogers Island Historical Association at campsites on Rogers Island, but this was the only belt axe found in the sutlers' area so it appears doubtful they were being sold by the merchants.

The early excavations on Rogers Island by the Rogers Island Historical Association recovered many axes, whetstones, saws, a grindstone, ice creepers, hoes, fishhooks, keys, inkwells, copper hospital pins, fishing sinkers, adzes, and ox shoes (Rogers Island Historical Association 1986:24–29). Later work on Rogers Island by Adirondack Community College (1991–1998) uncovered many of the same tool types, including four felling axes (fig. 5.2 and see Starbuck 2004:86), one belt axe, pole tips and pole support rings (see examples in fig. 5.3), ox shoes, horseshoes, and fishhooks. In addition, we found a superb fascine knife (figs. 5.4 and 5.5), four spades (one example appears in fig. 5.6), and even a complete tin bucket buried within a posthole (fig. 5.7). Given the great range of activities engaged in

FIG. 5.2. A felling axe discovered inside Dwelling 5 (an officers' house) on Rogers Island (ten inches long).

FIG. 5.3. An iron pole tip (left: 6 inches long) and an iron pole support ring (right: 2½ inches in diameter), both from campsites on Rogers Island.

FIG. 5.4. A fascine knife used for clearing brush, discovered in the dump next to the smallpox hospital on Rogers Island. Most of the wood handle has rotted away (22½ inches long).

FIG. 5.5. A closeup of the letters "LE" or "LL" on the blade of the fascine knife in fig. 5.4.

FIG. 5.6. The blade for a spade discovered inside the palisade trench around the smallpox hospital on Rogers Island. This had probably been abandoned when the blade broke away from its handle.

FIG. 5.7. A complete tin bucket discovered inside the posthole of a storehouse building on Rogers Island. The posthole had successfully preserved the shape of the bucket (eight inches tall and eight inches in diameter).

by soldiers, rangers, and officers as they built shelters, prepared their fires, cooked their food, and passed the time, it may truly be said that the artifacts on Rogers Island epitomize camp life for soldiers of the eighteenth-century British army as they waited to fight the French.

The McDougall Collection, assembled from the ruins of Fort Edward, contains an excellent assortment of tools used by the British army, including several axes (fig. 5.8), a fascine knife (fig. 5.8, bottom), several spades (fig. 5.9), and a gaff hook, a hook with chain, and pole tips (all in fig. 5.10). The McDougall Collection also contains wagon wheel rims and ox shoes (fig. 5.11), and even two ice creepers (fig. 5.12, left).

FIG. 5.8. Assorted axe heads and a fascine knife (the fascine knife at the bottom measures eighteen inches long). *From the McDougall Collection*

FIG. 5.9. The blades of some of the spades in the McDougall Collection in Fort Edward (left to right: 11¾ inches long, 16 inches long, 15¼ inches long, 13 inches long).

FIG. 5.10. Left to right: a gaff hook (12 inches long); three pole tips (left to right: 6 inches long, 4 inches long, 5½ inches long); and a hook with chain (hook is 9 inches long). *From the McDougall Collection*

FIG. 5.11. Wagon wheel rims (left: 11 inches long, right: 10⅝ inches long) and two ox shoes (center left: 5½ inches long and center right: 4½ inches long). *From the McDougall Collection*

FIG. 5.12. Fort Edward ice creepers. The two on the left are both from the McDougall Collection (top: 3½ inches long; bottom: 4 inches long); the two on the right were both discovered on the northern staircase in the sutling house (both are 3½ inches long).

Within the community of Lake George, the 1950s excavations at Fort William Henry uncovered an impressive assortment of tools, including a great many axes (figs. 5.13 and 5.14), numerous spades and shovels (one example of each appears in figs. 5.15 and 5.16), several hoes (one example appears in fig. 5.17), ice creepers, iron pole tips, and many ox shoes and horseshoes. The more recent work at Fort William Henry by Adirondack Community College (1997–2000) uncovered a variety of additional tools, including part of a grinding stone, four fishhooks, and two felling axes (Starbuck 2002b). Elsewhere in Lake George, metal detecting in the Birch Avenue area, south of the village, discovered two belt axes (fig. 5.18), and

FIG. 5.13. Axe heads excavated in the 1950s at Fort William Henry (top left: 9 inches long; top right: 8½ inches long; center left: 8½ inches long; center right: 8½ inches long; bottom: 9¼ inches long).

FIG. 5.14. Closeup of the British broad arrow mark (signifying government property) that appears on the blade of the axe in the top left of fig. 5.13.

FIG. 5.15. The metal cutting edge for a "shod" spade discovered during the 1950s' excavation at Fort William Henry (the cutting edge is 9⅜ inches wide). A single nail remains, evidence for how it was attached to the wood blade.

FIG. 5.16. One of several shovel blades excavated in the 1950s at Fort William Henry (11¼ inches long).

FIG. 5.17. One of several hoes excavated in the 1950s at Fort William Henry.

FIG. 5.18. Two belt axes discovered by collectors with metal detectors at military camps west of Route 9 at the south end of the village of Lake George (top: 5 inches long; bottom: 5⁵⁄₁₆ inches long).

FIG. 5.19. A hinge, probably from an officer's chest, discovered inside the northernmost barracks foundation (an officers' barracks) at the Lake George Battlefield Park. It is labeled with the name "Ahmuty" and is the only personalized artifact that we have discovered in any of the sites in Lake George or Fort Edward (3¾ inches long).

excavations in the Lake George Battlefield Park (2000–2001), while not finding very many tools, recovered a personalized hinge from a chest within a possible officers' barracks, almost unique in that a name, "Ahmuty," was inscribed into the metal (fig. 5.19).

Each one of these sites also contains a variety of small items that may not technically be "tools." These include such things as pothooks, bandage pins, and lead sinkers for fishing, all of which would have been necessary to the functioning of the camps and forts. Many of these are difficult to place within a single, most appropriate chapter. For example, brass compasses—which were critical for military maneuvers and for determining camp layout—have been placed in chapter 3 as "Weaponry." They could have been included just as easily in this chapter as an example of "tools."

The Sutling House

Because the Fort Edward sutling house was a residence, and not just a tavern or place of business, it is difficult to interpret whether any of the tools discovered there were actually being sold there. However, a review of the "tools and equipment" in the appendix reveals quantities of just "1" or "2" for most tool categories in the sutling house. There were just one felling axe, one belt axe, three chisels, one hammerhead, one blade from a spade, one cutting edge from a shod spade, two ice creepers, two files, three whetstones, two punches, one stirrup, two horseshoes, two padlocks, eight keys, a brass chatelaine with chain, a lead weight created by flattening a musket ball, and a brass clasp (fastener) from a book (figs. 5.1, 5.12 [right], 5.20, 5.21, 5.22, 5.23, and 5.24). The only categories of "tools or equipment"

FIG. 5.20. Various tools found in the Fort Edward sutling house: a felling axe (top left: 8 inches long); the belt axe pictured in fig. 5.1 (center left: 5 inches long); a wedge (bottom left: 4½ inches long); a hammerhead (top right: 5 inches long); and an iron stirrup (lower right: 4¾ inches wide and 4½ inches tall).

FIG. 5.21. The blade for a spade that was discovered on the cellar floor of the sutling house in Fort Edward (11¾ inches long and 6½ inches wide).

FIG. 5.22. The metal cutting edge for a "shod" spade that lay on the cellar floor of the sutling house in Fort Edward. This would have been attached to a wood blade, now rotted away. (The cutting edge is nine inches wide.)

FIG. 5.23. An iron padlock (left: 3⅛ inches long) and several iron keys discovered inside the sutling house in Fort Edward.

FIG. 5.24. Left to right: a lead weight (or possibly a one-hole button for a leather thong), created by hammering a musket ball to flatten it (1⅜ inches diameter; 28.5 grams); a brass thimble (11/16 inch high and ½ inch in diameter); a heart-shaped brass chatelaine with chain (1⅜ inches long by 1 inch wide); and a brass book clasp (2⅛ inches long), all discovered inside the sutling house in Fort Edward.

in the sutling house that were more frequent were ox shoes (twelve), fragments of wagon wheel hardware (forty-eight), and barrel hoop fragments (fifty-six) (fig. 5.25), all of which pertain to the transport to and storage of commodities within the house—they were not goods to be sold. Curiously enough, there was no evidence for equipment with which to measure or weigh supplies or foodstuffs that were being sold from the house.

Tools thus do not appear to have been a significant part of the stores within the sutling house, and if these tools were in fact simply used within the house, then the sutlers had barely enough tools for themselves. This reinforces the interpretation that the sutlers in this house were quite specialized in the commodities they sold, chiefly selling the "vices" of alcohol and tobacco, and they may well have left it up to other merchants to sell something as practical as "tools" to the British army!

FIG. 5.25. Matthew Rozell removing one of the many barrel hoops discovered inside the cellar of the sutling house in Fort Edward.

"Went into ye Fort For Some Nails"
—Jabez Fitch, Jr.
(June 2, 1757)

6

Architectural Hardware

General Overview

NAILS AND WINDOW GLASS are among the most abundant materials recovered on all historic archeological digs, as are brick fragments from chimneys and fireplaces. The distribution of pintles and hinges, door latch hardware, and door locks is always extremely helpful in determining a building's construction details and the location of such features as doors. Still, many of our military structures in Fort Edward and Lake George were relatively impermanent, often lacking niceties such as windows, and architectural hardware tends to be more concentrated within barracks buildings and other relatively substantial structures.

Earl Stott's excavations on Rogers Island did recover some hinges and door latches (Rogers Island Historical Association 1986:29–30), and one of his most interesting finds was a period brick with the date "1759" inscribed by hand on one side (before the brick had been fired). A similar brick is contained within the McDougall Collection from Moon Street in Fort Edward, also with the finger-incised date of "1759" (fig. 6.1). This brick is among materials collected from within the foundations of barracks buildings, and the McDougall Collection also contains several substantial strap hinges (fig. 6.2), as well as a lock plate and some iron keys.

The extensive excavations on Rogers Island by Adirondack Community College (1991–1998) uncovered a total of just ten hinges and fewer than five hundred fragments of window glass (Starbuck 2004). Most of these excavations were at the sites of tents and huts, and clearly these types of temporary structures contain very little by way of windows, hinges or door latches. Starbuck has discussed in detail the range of vernacular building types on Rogers Island (Starbuck 2004:chapter 5), and even the foundations of barracks on the island have little by way of surviving architectural hardware,

FIG. 6.1. A brick made in Fort Edward with the finger-incised date of 1759 (7¼ by 3½ by 2 inches). *From the McDougall Collection.*

FIG. 6.2. Iron strap hinges (top to bottom: 18⅛ inches long, 19½ inches long, 9⅜ inches long); two iron keys (left to right: 3⅞ inches long, 5¼ inches long); and an iron lock plate (bottom right: 5⅝ inches tall), all from Fort Edward. *From the McDougall Collection.*

perhaps because much salvaging was subsequently done inside the buildings by early settlers.

The very substantial excavations at Fort William Henry in the 1950s recovered large numbers of bricks and much building hardware from the ruins of barracks buildings, and numerous examples of hinges and other hardware are on display within the reconstructed fort. Our own more limited excavations at the fort in the 1990s, through Adirondack Community College, focused more on the contents of dumps than on uncovering substantial buildings, and we recovered only a few hinge fragments, a single door handle, a single lock plate, and minimal window glass. Most of this material derived from the ruins of the West Barracks (Starbuck 2002b).

Our excavations into barracks foundations at the Lake George Battlefield

FIG. 6.3. A door lock found inside a barracks foundation at the Lake George Battlefield Park ($8\frac{5}{16}$ inches long and $4\frac{11}{16}$ inches wide).

FIG. 6.4. An iron door latch recovered from a barracks foundation at the Lake George Battlefield Park ($5\frac{11}{16}$ inches long).

FIG. 6.5. An "HL" hinge discovered inside the northernmost barracks foundation (an officers' barracks) at the Lake George Battlefield Park ($8\frac{1}{8}$ inches long and $7\frac{3}{16}$ inches wide).

Park (2001–2001) were much more successful in revealing significant architectural material, including extensive brick concentrations, much plaster (within the northernmost barracks building), door locks (fig. 6.3), an iron door latch (fig. 6.4), and a very large example of an "HL" hinge that was substantial enough to carry the weight of a very good-sized door (fig. 6.5). The lack of previous archeology at the Battlefield Park, coupled with quite

FIG. 6.6. Examples of door pintles found in the sutling house in Fort Edward (top to bottom: 3 inches long, 4½ inches long, 4½ inches long, 5 inches long, 5¼ inches long).

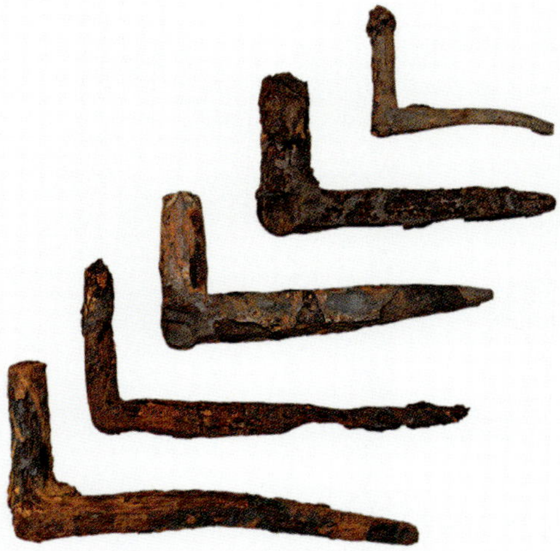

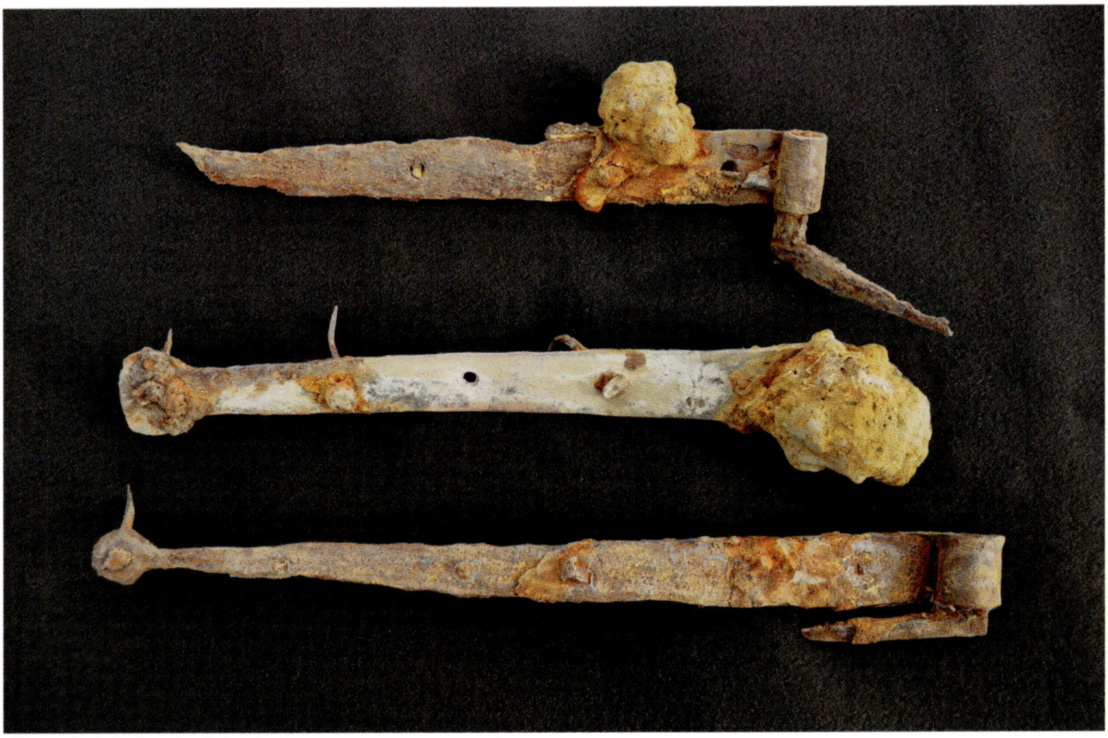

FIG. 6.7. Three iron hinges, among the many found in the sutling house in Fort Edward (top to bottom: 12 inches long, fourteen inches long, fifteen inches long).

FIG. 6.8. A latch bar catch found inside the sutling house in Fort Edward (4⅞ inches long).

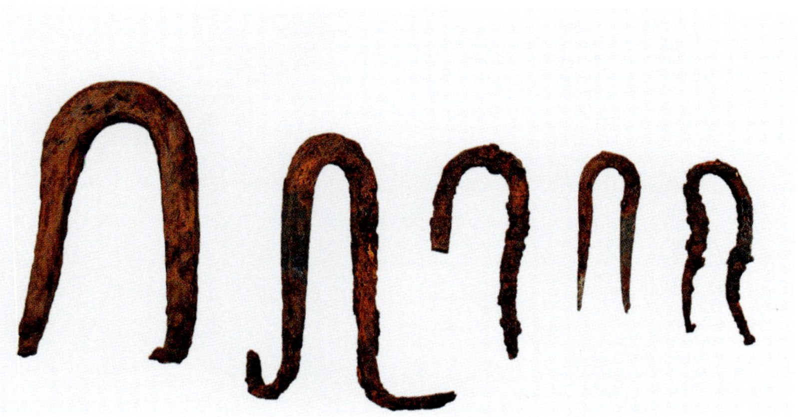

FIG. 6.9. Representative staples (driven into wood) found in the sutling house in Fort Edward (left to right: 4¼ inches long, 4 inches long, 3¼ inches long, 2½ inches long, 2¾ inches long).

limited looting by collectors, appears to have successfully preserved some very pristine architectural remains.

The Sutling House

The solid construction and relative permanence of the sutling house in Fort Edward resulted in a wealth of architectural hardware, and we recovered much more material than at any of our previous excavation sites. Our excavations recorded 8,078 rose head nails, 3,512 fragments of window glass, eight pintles (fig. 6.6), a ninth pintle still attached to its hinge, twenty-six hinge fragments (fig. 6.7), a separate shutter hinge, a thumb latch, a latch plate, a latch bar catch (fig. 6.8), and even fourteen large iron staples of varying sizes (fig. 6.9). These finds were scattered throughout the cellar hole, interspersed with the burned remains of boards and joists.

Bricks lay everywhere within the house, but principally at the northern and southern ends of the cellar where fireplaces and chimneys had collapsed. Virtually hundreds of bricks had fallen into every available cavity,

FIG. 6.10. Wrought iron hooks found just a few feet apart in a scatter of brick fragments in the west-center of the sutling house in Fort Edward (top: 4⅝ inches long, still embedded in brick; bottom: 7 inches long). These hooks may have been used to suspend pots over a fire.

including the northern staircase, which was positively filled with the bricks of the fallen chimney. On the western side of the cellar, at roughly the midway point, two substantial wrought iron hooks were discovered side by side on the edge of a different brick scatter, suggesting that pots were meant to hang there in an oven area (fig. 6.10).

As artifact conservation proceeds on the contents of the sutling house, and as computerized mapping is conducted of the nails, hinges, and brick concentrations found within the cellar, it should be possible to map out quite precisely the locations of doorways and other architectural features. The sutling house thus has the potential to become our best understood structure within any of the New York military camps.

> *"This Morning I Swopt Shoe Buckels with Corpl Thos Andrus"*
> —Jabez Fitch, Jr.
> (June 28, 1757)

7

Personal Artifacts

Clothing, Sewing, and Grooming

General Overview

NOTHING is as "personal" to an archeologist as the buttons, buckles, and cufflinks that soldiers and officers wore on their uniforms, forever reminding us of their individual choices and giving us a taste of how they actually may have "looked" while they served their country. These items were easily lost, and they are found with frequency at eighteenth-century sites. Most of the buttons of the French and Indian War were of brass, and the numbered, regimental buttons that characterized forces of the American Revolution (and later) had not yet appeared. Buttons of wood, bone, and shell tended to be undecorated, but many of the brass buttons were undecorated as well. (See Troiani 2001 for an excellent overview of buttons of the American Revolution.)

Actual remains of clothing tend to be extremely rare at northern military sites, but evidence for sewing is sometimes present in the form of thimbles, needles, and pins. Combs are fairly rare, and most are carved from bone, the so-called "lice combs" that no doubt were beneficial to personal hygiene!

The work conducted on Rogers Island by Earl Stott beginning in 1960 recovered great numbers of buttons, buckles, and cufflinks, and in one location Stott believed he had located "the site of a regimental tailor's shop" because of the number of buttons, accompanied by a thimble and a pair of scissors (see Rogers Island Historical Association 1986:28). Later work on the island by Adirondack Community College had similar success, resulting in the discovery of one hundred and thirty-one metal buttons (figs. 7.1 and 7.2), two wood buttons, eight bone buttons (fig. 7.3), sixteen dress buckles (7.4), thirteen cufflinks (fig. 7.5), and a single brass tinkler that probably hung from the fringe of a garment (fig. 7.6). One pair of sew-

FIG. 7.1. Representative brass and pewter buttons (obverse sides) discovered on Rogers Island.

FIG. 7.2. Representative brass and pewter buttons (reverses of those pictured in fig. 7.1).

FIG. 7.3. One-hole bone buttons discovered in a latrine on Rogers Island (each is ½ inch in diameter). These were typically worn on male undergarments or on women's clothing.

FIG. 7.4. Representative brass dress buckles discovered on Rogers Island. The upper right buckle is a shoe buckle, and the rest are knee buckles.

FIG. 7.5. A pair of brass cufflinks discovered on Rogers Island (each is ½ inch in diameter).

FIG. 7.6. A triangular brass tinkler with a single punched hole, probably meant to be hung from clothing. This was discovered at the Smallpox Hospital on Rogers Island (one inch wide and one inch tall).

FIG. 7.7. Rusted iron scissors excavated from the remains of Dwelling 5 (an officers' house) on Rogers Island (five inches long).

FIG. 7.8. Two strips of gold braid discovered in 1998 inside Dwelling 5 (the remains of an officers' house) on Rogers Island.

ing scissors (fig. 7.7), six pins, and two thimbles provided modest evidence for sewing on the island, but by far the most exciting discovery came in the form of two pieces of gold braid, the trim from a uniform. These were found together inside the foundation of Dwelling 5 (an officers' house) on Rogers Island (fig. 7.8).

The McDougall Collection from the ruins of Fort Edward contains a rich assortment of dress buckles (fig. 7.9), metal buttons, and even two inscribed razor handles (fig. 7.9, bottom row). The 1995–1996 excavation at that fort, by Adirondack Community College, also recovered several brass dress buckles and a large brass coat button inscribed with the name "Georgius II Rex." However, these are very small samples when compared to the personal artifacts recovered during the 1950s excavation at Fort William Henry. The Fort William Henry Museum exhibits large numbers of buttons and buckles, many more examples are in storage there, and to these may be added a sizeable collection excavated from the fort by Adirondack Community College (ACC) in the 1990s. The ACC excavation recovered eighty-eight metal buttons, three wood buttons, one bone button, twenty-four dress buckles, eight cufflinks, and a single plain finger ring, as well as modest evidence for sewing. Two pairs of sewing scissors, one brass thimble, one

needle, and twenty-five pins were located at various sites on the grounds, but these came chiefly from within the foundation of the West Barracks (fig. 7.10).

Elsewhere in Lake George, amateur metal detecting in the vicinity of Birch Avenue recovered six metal buttons and six brass buckles, and the ACC 2000–2001 excavations in the Lake George Battlefield Park discovered a variety of buckles, buttons (fig. 7.11), two stock clasps (one example appears in fig. 7.12), clothing hooks and eyes, cufflinks, and two pairs of sewing scissors (figs. 7.13 and 7.14). (For comparable eighteenth-century examples of scissors, see Beaudry 2006:127.) Most impressively, one of the barracks foundations in the Battlefield Park also contained a single strip of gold braid (fig. 7.15), bringing the total number of pieces of braid to just three after eighteen years of digging at many different military sites in the Fort Edward and Lake George area.

FIG. 7.9. Assorted brass dress buckles and utility buckles (top three rows) and inscribed razor handles (bottom row), all from the McDougall Collection in Fort Edward. Both razor handles are 3¼ inches long; the bottom left handle reads SUCCESS TO THE KING OF PRUSSIA and the bottom right handle reads I SAY FOR EVER HUS A.

FIG. 7.10. A brass thimble (center), needle (left), and pin (right) excavated from the foundation of the West Barracks at Fort William Henry in the 1990s.

FIG. 7.11. A brass button excavated at the Lake George Battlefield Park (one inch in diameter). *Courtesy of the New York State Department of Environmental Conservation.*

FIG. 7.12. A brass neck stock clasp (2 by 1⅛ inches), one of two discovered at the Lake George Battlefield Park.

FIG. 7.13. Sewing scissors discovered at the Lake George Battlefield Park (5⅛ inches long).

FIG. 7.14. Sewing scissors (the two sides have been separated by rust) recovered from the Lake George Battlefield Park (5⅛ inches long).

FIG. 7.15. Gold braid excavated in 2000 from a barracks foundation at the Lake George Battlefield Park (six inches long). *Courtesy of the New York State Department of Environmental Conservation.*

The Sutling House

The sutling house in Fort Edward contained a wonderful variety of personal and clothing-related artifacts, and these were easily among the most interesting contents of the house. There were seventy buckles of various types (fig. 7.16), one hundred and twelve buttons of brass, pewter, wood, bone,

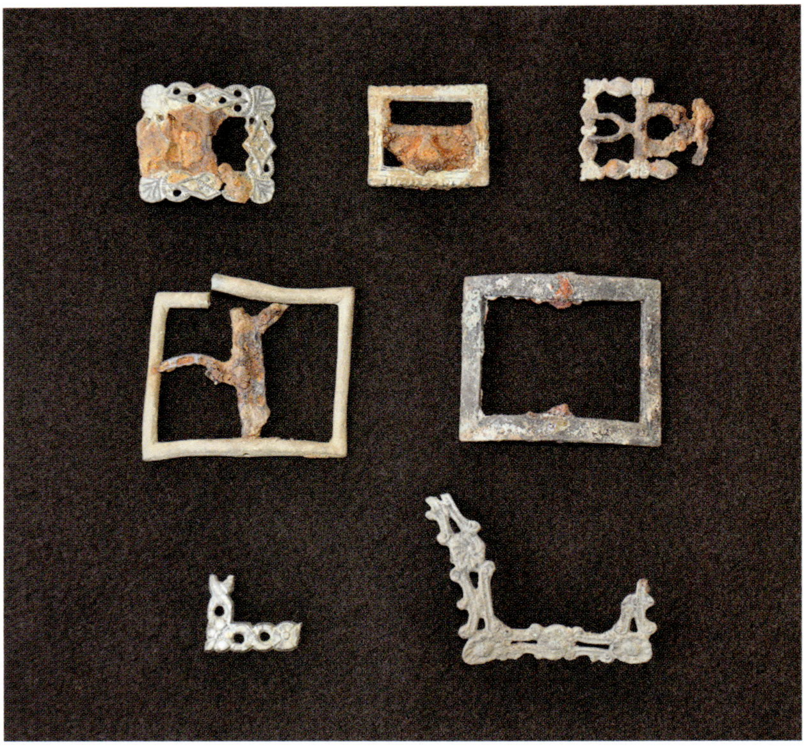

FIG. 7.16. Representative brass dress buckles discovered in the cellar of the sutling house in Fort Edward. The smaller buckles (top row and bottom left) are knee buckles, and the larger buckles (middle row and bottom right) are shoe buckles.

and shell (examples appear in fig. 7.17), plus one numbered regimental button that was probably intrusive from a later date.

Our excavations at military encampments have rarely recovered more than a cufflink or two from within a single structure, but the Fort Edward sutling house contained a fascinating selection of cufflinks (figs. 7.18 and 7.19), consisting of:

2 pairs of cufflinks (1 pair has clear glass insets; 1 pair is all-brass)
3 single cufflinks (with clear glass insets)
2 single cufflinks (with jet insets)
2 single cufflinks (with green glass insets)
1 single brass cufflink

Clothing fasteners (hooks and eyes) have been quite rare at all of our excavation sites, but the sutling house contained a total of ninety-four clothing hooks and eyes (examples appear in fig. 7.20). Nearly all of these were made of iron, but three very small clothing hooks were made of brass. The vast majority of the fasteners were found just outside the northern cellar door of the house, perhaps the contents of a box that was dropped just as the occupants ran from the burning house.

Four fine-toothed bone comb fragments were also found within the sut-

FIG. 7.17. Representative brass and pewter buttons discovered in the Fort Edward sutling house.

FIG. 7.18. Brass cufflinks (sleeve links) with glass insets discovered in the Fort Edward sutling house. (All are ½ inch in diameter.)

FIG. 7.19. Jet glass insets for cufflinks (top row) and green glass insets (bottom row), all from the Fort Edward sutling house. (All are ⅜ to ⅝ inch in diameter.)

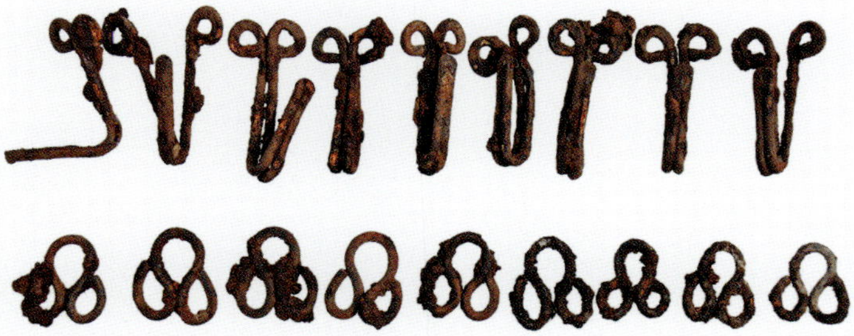

FIG. 7.20. Iron clothing fasteners found just outside the northern cellar entrance of the sutling house in Fort Edward. (Hooks are in the top row and eyes in the bottom row.) Hooks average about 1½ inches long, and eyes measure about ¾ inch long by ¾ inch wide. Only three fasteners (not pictured here) were made of brass.

FIG. 7.21. Fragments of bone combs with very fine teeth, often referred to as lice combs. These were found inside the sutling house in Fort Edward (left: 2 5/16 inches long; right: 1 3/8 inches wide and 1 inch long).

lers' cellar hole, and two of these are depicted in fig. 7.21. All were quite fragile and broken into rather small pieces, and one of these was a foldable comb (fig. 7.21, left). Given such a small sample, it is impossible to state whether combs were being sold from the sutling house. Also, because only one brass thimble was found within the house (fig. 5.24, second from left), it seems doubtful that sewing supplies were among the commodities being sold there. All the same, in comparing these findings to other sites we have excavated, it appears reasonably certain that the sutlers were selling buttons, buckles, cufflinks, and clothing fasteners from their establishment, and we are left wondering, "What items of cloth or clothing did they sell as well?" Unfortunately, no fragments of cloth have survived, most likely due to the acidity of the soil and the annual flooding of the cellar hole.

"*I Recd 2S [shillings] For my Days work*"
—Jabez Fitch, Jr.
(June 4, 1757)

8

Coins

General Overview

MID-EIGHTEENTH-CENTURY commerce was conducted with a combination of British and Spanish currency (fig. 8.1), and the Spanish milled dollar (valued at eight reales) was a mainstay in the American colonies (Yeoman 2009:10). While there is an enormous body of literature that describes early American currency (e.g., Mossman 1993), this literature is not based on archeologically derived material, and Fort Michilimackinac is one of very few military sites for which the examinations of coins discovered archeologically have been published in detail (Heldman 1980).

FIG. 8.1. It doesn't get any more exciting than this! A crew chief on the Fort Edward dig, Brittany Hastings, has just discovered a Spanish coin inside the cellar of the sutling house.

Coinage within the military camps in Lake George and Fort Edward is remarkably similar in that every site contains a scattering of low-denomination English copper coins (half-pence and farthings), and nearly comparable numbers of Spanish silver coins (cobs, half-real milled coins, one-real milled coins, and one-bit pieces of eight). There are few coins of any other denomination and virtually no English silver coins. England had chronic shortages of coins throughout the colonial period, and the English mercantile system was infamous for allowing as few coins as possible to go to its colonies. Consequently, the frequency of Spanish silver at our archeological sites was not a surprise. Paper currency, while printed by some of the colonies, has not survived archeologically, and few coins minted in the colonies have been found.

The excavations on Rogers Island that were directed by Earl Stott and the Rogers Island Historical Association between 1960 and the late 1980s (Rogers Island Historical Association 1986; Adler 1986) recovered literally hundreds of Spanish and British coins. Earl Stott proudly displayed large numbers of these coins to anyone who visited Rogers Island, and the fre-

FIG. 8.2. British half-pence (left), 1734, from Rogers Island and Spanish one-real milled coin (right), 1751, found inside the remains of the smallpox hospital on Rogers Island.

FIG. 8.3. A Spanish silver cob (right) and a Spanish silver four-reales coin (left) from a hut (Site 19), both found on Rogers Island.

quency of coins helps to suggest that a lively cash economy was present at the Fort Edward military camps. Soldiers' diaries in Fort Edward describe frequent purchases, and 15,000 men constituted an enormous number of consumers.

Our own excavations on Rogers Island between 1991 and 1998 (Starbuck 1995, 1997a, 2004) recovered some twenty period coins, consisting of fourteen British half-pence and six Spanish reales and cobs (examples appear in figs. 8.2 and 8.3). These were scattered throughout huts, barracks, and dumps, and some were even located at the site of the smallpox hospital on the island. It is doubtful that soldiers and officers carried very many coins on their persons, and with thousands of men living in a restricted area, it also seems doubtful that a coin would have gone missing for long. However, coins were perhaps lost in tall grass or sandy soil, not easily recoverable except with the modern sifting screens used by archeologists!

The density of coins on Rogers Island is really quite amazing when compared to other area sites. Our work at Fort William Henry between 1997 and 2000 recovered only five British half-pence and two Spanish reales (an example appears in fig. 8.4), and excavations at the fort in Fort Edward and the Lake George Battlefield Park recovered only a few coins at each site.

The Sutling House

Set against this background, the sutling house in Fort Edward proved to be an exceptionally good source of period coins (seventy-one of them), reflective of the buying and selling that was the principal function of that building (see appendix). Many of these coins were found just outside the door leading to the northern staircase of the sutling house, but other coins were

FIG. 8.4. A Spanish silver one-half real coin, 1735, discovered during the 1990s' excavation at Fort William Henry.

FIG. 8.5. The obverse of a 1652 Massachusetts Oak Tree Shilling discovered on the cellar floor of the Fort Edward sutling house (1 1/16 inch in diameter).

FIG. 8.6. The reverse of the Oak Tree Shilling in fig. 8.5.

recovered from throughout the cellar hole and in surrounding dumps. The earliest coin was an example of colonial currency, a silver Oak Tree Shilling (Noe 14), thin and rather worn, and with a small hole drilled through it for hanging (figs. 8.5 and 8.6). All Oak Tree Shillings were minted in Massachusetts with the same date (1652), and "The 1680s–1690s are usually suggested for the end of the coinage based on some documentary evidence, but the coinage seems to have continued to circulate in quantity into the eighteenth century" (Oliver Hoover, personal communication, June 28, 2007). Was this Oak Tree Shilling hung around the neck of our sutler, or was it perhaps nailed up over the fireplace at the northern end of the sutling house? (It was found amid the brick rubble from the fireplace.) Given its age, there is also the possibility that it simply was retained as a good luck charm by the occupants of the house.

FIG. 8.7. A 1695 French liard found inside the sutling house in Fort Edward (7/8 inch in diameter).

The next oldest coin to be discovered was a 1695 French liard with the bust of King Louis XIV on the obverse side of the coin (fig. 8.7). The discovery of this copper coin in the sutling house was somewhat unexpected because no other French coins have been found at any of our other dig sites in Fort Edward or Lake George. It may well date to the earlier period of commerce conducted between the Dutch trader John Henry Lydius and the French and Indians to the north (Hamilton 1964).

British copper half-pence were the most common form of currency at the sutling house, as well as at every other site we have examined. We found thirty-eight of these coins, and while about half were badly corroded and unreadable, suggesting a lengthy period of circulation, the remainder bore the dates of 1714, 1718, 1721, 1723, 1727, 1730, 1731, 1734, 1738 (two coins), 1739 (two coins), 1745, 1748, 1749 (three coins), 1755, and 1756 (fig. 8.8). Four British copper farthings were also recovered (fig. 8.8, bottom row),

FIG. 8.8. British copper half-pence (top four rows) and British farthings (bottom row), all from the sutling house in Fort Edward. These are the best-preserved examples of British copper coinage from that site; all others (not pictured here) were worn and corroded beyond recognition.

FIG. 8.9. Spanish silver cob money found inside the sutling house in Fort Edward.

FIG. 8.10. Spanish silver milled coins, one-half real (top row) and one real (bottom row), all from the sutling house in Fort Edward.

bearing the dates of 1724, 1736, and 1739 (no date could be read on the fourth farthing). There were no British coins of larger denominations.

Spanish cob money, created by cutting the coin from a rolled silver bar and striking it with a crude die and hammer, appeared next in frequency, and there were sixteen of these (fig. 8.9). Most cobs were one real in value, although we recovered one half-real cob and one four-real cob. Eight milled or "pillar" coins were discovered, and of these there were three one-real coins with the dates of 1744, 1746, and 1750, and there were five half-real

FIG. 8.11. Spanish silver one-bit pieces of eight (a cut fraction of an eight-reales coin) discovered inside the sutling house in Fort Edward. Two bear the mint mark "M" (for Mexico City).

coins with the dates of 1738, 1740, 1745, 1746, and 1756 (fig. 8.10). We also found three one-bit pieces of eight in the sutling house, and these had all been cut from larger eight-reales coins (fig. 8.11). These bore the initials "MF," representing the assayers Manuel de Leon and Francisco de la Pena y Flores, who operated from 1731 to 1754. The mint mark "Mo," which stands for Mexico City, appears to the left of the date on all of these coins. According to Oliver Hoover, "the cobs seem to mainly come from Potosi, whereas the identifiable milled pieces all come from Mexico" (personal communication, February 2, 2006). All of the Spanish coins were in excellent condition, in stark contrast with the corroded British coppers.

9

"in ye Evening There was
a Fiddle Going vary
Brisk in ye Camp"
—Jabez Fitch, Jr.
(May 29, 1757)

Miscellany

Glass Trade Beads, Musical Instruments, and Tobacco Pipes

Glass Beads

NONE OF OUR EXCAVATIONS on Rogers Island, or within the ruins of Fort Edward or Fort William Henry, produced a single glass trade bead. However, four examples, each of a different style and color (fig. 9.1), were discovered in the sutlers' camp in Fort Edward between 2001 and 2008, and an additional two beads in 2009 (not pictured). Three of the beads in fig. 9.1 are probably Venetian, had very long periods of manufacture and circulation, and cannot definitively be attributed to either Lydius or the sutlers. The fourth, which is bright navy and hexagonal (fig. 9.1, lower left), is Bohemian, clearly post-1800, and does not pertain to the colonial wars (Karlis Karklins, Personal Communication, Jan. 9, 2009). While the continuous use of a sifting screen with finer mesh might have discovered additional examples, we nevertheless shifted over to finer screens whenever beads were found, and at no time did this recover any additional beads.

With time, we came to assume that beads did not exist in appreciable

FIG. 9.1. Glass trade beads from the vicinity of the sutling house in Fort Edward. Top left: tubular, opaque red over transparent green core; Kidd System: IIIa3 (very long time range; as early as 1590 up to ca. 1830) (½ inch long and ⅛ inch in diameter). Top right: round, light gray; Kidd System: IIa9 (very long-lived) (⅛ inch in diameter). Lower left: tubular, cornerless hexagonal, bright navy over oyster white core; Kidd System: IIIf* (no number) (definitely post 1800) (¼ inch long and ¼ inch in diameter). Lower right: wound, bright navy, round (oblate); Kidd System: WIb16 (very long time range; late 1600s/early 1700s up until the twentieth century) (3⁄16 inch in diameter). *Identifications courtesy of Karlis Karklins.*

FIG. 9.2. Examples of glass seed beads (and a few larger beads) recovered from an outworks of Fort Edward in 2009. All were found by sieving the soil through fine window mesh. Diameters of the beads generally ranged between about 2.2 and 2.8 mm, and their bore diameters averaged about 0.59 mm. *Elizabeth Hall, Personal Communication, August 2009.*

numbers in British camps of northern New York in the 1750s, so we were totally surprised in the summer of 2009 when we dug into an outworks of Fort Edward—only about 500 feet south of the sutling house—and discovered two large glass beads plus fifty-eight small glass seed beads (examples appear in fig. 9.2). For centuries seed beads have been sewn into patterns on clothing, moccasins, or sashes as a colorful decoration, and their very small size does make them rather difficult to recover archeologically. Those discovered in 2009 were retrieved only by sieving through fine window screen, and they were chiefly white and off white, although a few were green, brown, red, or gray in color.

The likely interpretation of this patterning is that the British sutlers in Fort Edward and Lake George during the 1750s did not stock or sell beads. If they had been engaged in the extensive trade in glass beads to Native Americans that is richly represented at other, earlier sites throughout the Northeast, then there would have been many more beads in evidence. Still, our 2009 discovery does raise the question of whether we might have finally recovered evidence for John Henry Lydius's earlier trading network with Native Americans in northern New York and Canada (Hamilton 1964). We may well have found a trading site that dates to ten or twenty years earlier than the 1750s' fort construction, a camp that was built over when British forces arrived.

Musical Instruments

The simple Jew's harp, also referred to as a "jaw harp" or "mouth harp," has been in existence since at least the third century B.C., and its shape has evolved considerably over time (Kolltviet 2006). It truly is one of the simplest of all musical instruments—a small, flexible tongue attached to a frame—and its tongue is placed in the player's mouth and plucked with a finger to make the sound. In doing so, the jaw and mouth act as a resonator, and the pitch may be altered by changing the shape of the mouth.

The Jew's harp is perhaps the clearest archeological indicator of a "leisure" activity on the part of the British soldiers, and Gary Zaboly has observed that "Clay pipes, chewing tobacco and snuff helped while away the rare hours of relaxation [for Rogers' Rangers], as did impromptu singing or concerts with fiddle and jew's harp" (Zaboly 2004:151).

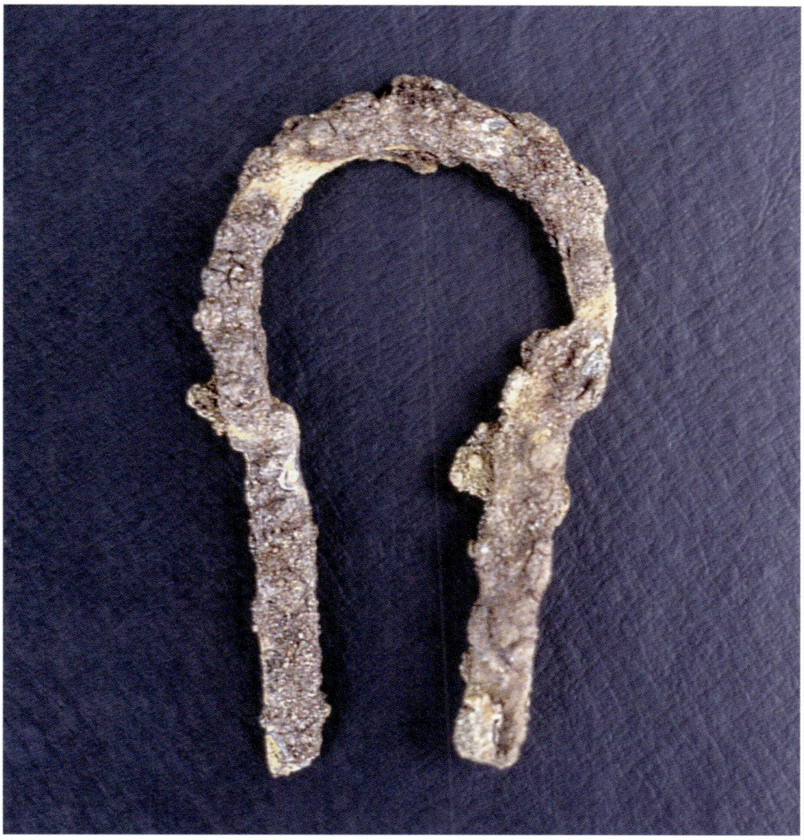

FIG. 9.3. Iron Jew's harp recovered from the dump east of Fort William Henry during the 1990s' excavation (2 13/16 inches long).

FIG. 9.4. Iron Jew's harp excavated from the fort in Fort Edward in 1995 (1¾ inches long and 1¼ inches wide).

FIG. 9.5. Top row: Iron Jew's harps (jaw harps, mouth harps) on the left and right; brass Jew's harp in the center, all from the sutling house in Fort Edward. None has retained its metal tongue that permitted the instrument to play notes when placed in the performer's mouth. (Left to right: 1¾ inches long, 2¼ inches long, 2 inches long.) Bottom row: A bone whistle or flute worked from a sheep metapodial, found inside the fort in Fort Edward (4⅜ inches long).

The Jew's harp has been located, in very modest numbers, at most of the military sites in Lake George and Fort Edward. Two examples, both made of iron, were excavated from the dump (Site 5) on the eastern side of Fort William Henry in the 1990s (one is illustrated in fig. 9.3); one of iron was recovered from that fort in the 1950s; one of iron came from the excavation of the fort in Fort Edward in 1995 (fig. 9.4); and one Jew's harp of brass was discovered during the Fort Gage excavation in 1975 (Starbuck 1999b:117).

Compared to these other excavations, the Jew's harp was unusually well represented at the sutling house in Fort Edward because four examples were recovered, three of iron and one of brass (Stafford type) (three of the four are depicted in fig. 9.5, top row). While the sample is small, this may well mean that the Jew's harp was one of the commodities being sold in the sutling house.

The only other musical instrument to be recovered archeologically was a bone whistle or flute, discovered at the site of the fort in Fort Edward in 2002 and made from the metapodial of a sheep (fig. 9.5, bottom). The proximal end had been cut away, and a notch was cut midway down the shaft of the bone, allowing the player to blow across the open hole.

Tobacco Pipes

The smoking of tobacco in white clay pipes was a favorite leisure activity throughout the military camps in Fort Edward and Lake George, and pipe stem and bowl fragments are to be found just about everywhere. The bowls of these long-stemmed, molded pipes often have the maker's marks (and sometimes the cartouche) of either Robert Tippet ("RT") of Bristol or William Mamby ("WM") of London. Our excavations on Rogers Island recovered nine hundred and fifteen stem fragments (4/64 inch was the most common stem hole diameter) (fig. 9.6), and the 1990s excavations at Fort William Henry discovered 1,071 stem fragments (and once again, 4/64 inch was the most common stem hole diameter). Two boxes of tobacco pipes

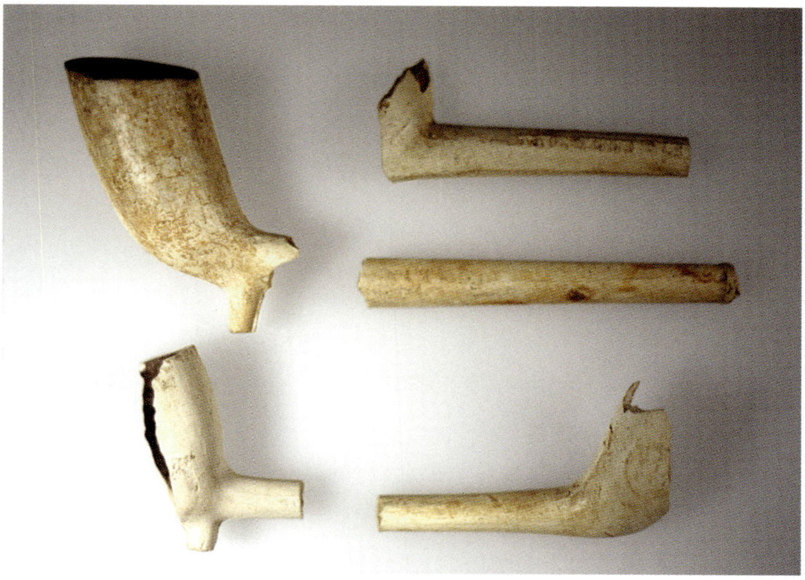

FIG. 9.6. Representative tobacco pipes recovered from Rogers Island. The pipe in the lower right bears the maker's mark of "WM" (for William Mamby of London, England).

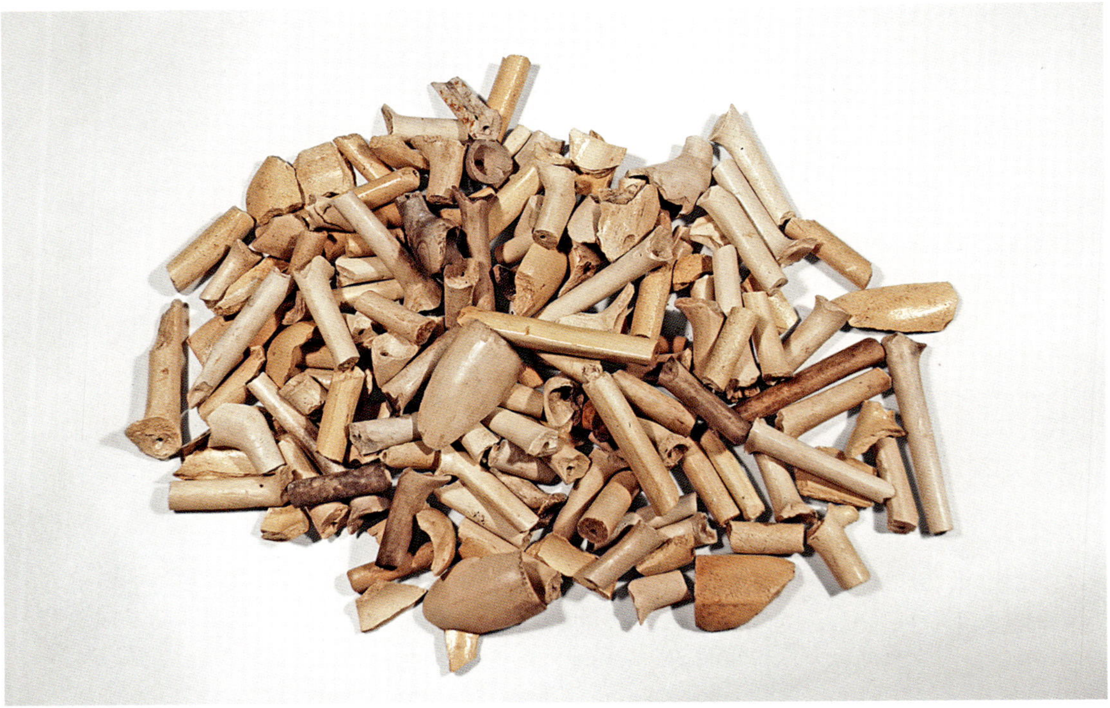

FIG. 9.7. A sampling of the tobacco pipe stems and bowls discovered at Fort William Henry during the 1950s' excavations of the fort.

FIG. 9.8. Exposing a large cache of tobacco pipes on the cellar floor of the sutling house in Fort Edward. No traces remained of the keg or box that once contained these pipes, and none showed any signs of having been smoked. Many bore the maker's mark "RT" (for Robert Tippet of Bristol, England).

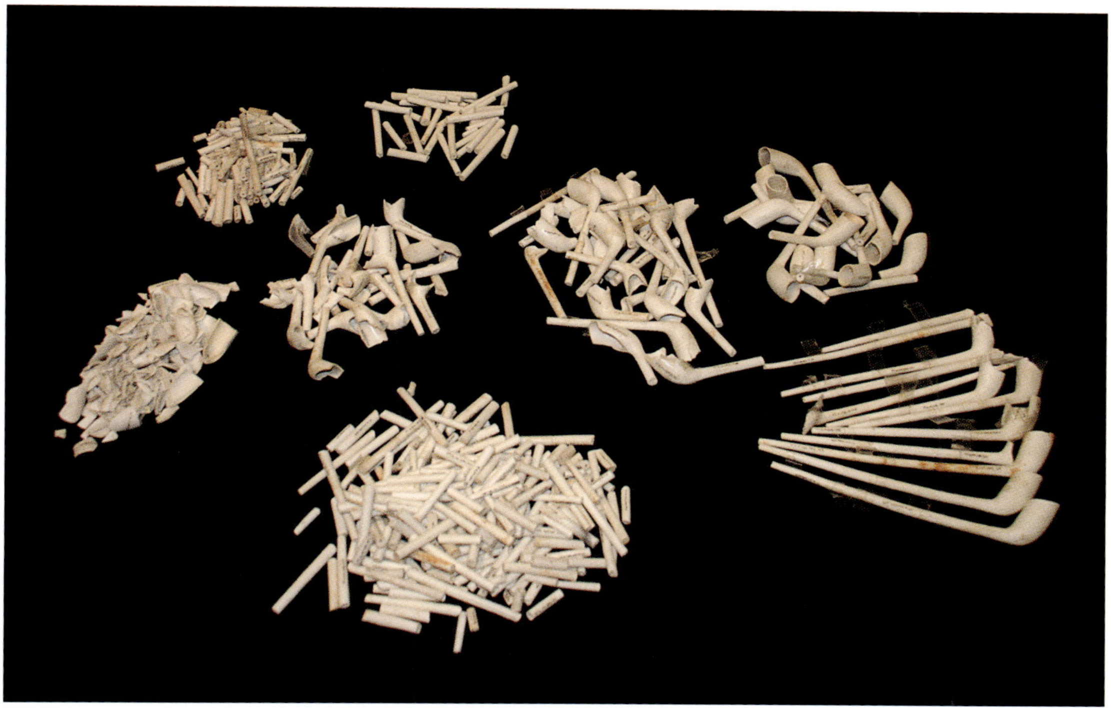

FIG. 9.9. Piles of tobacco pipe stems and bowls from the Fort Edward sutling house, waiting to be glued together.

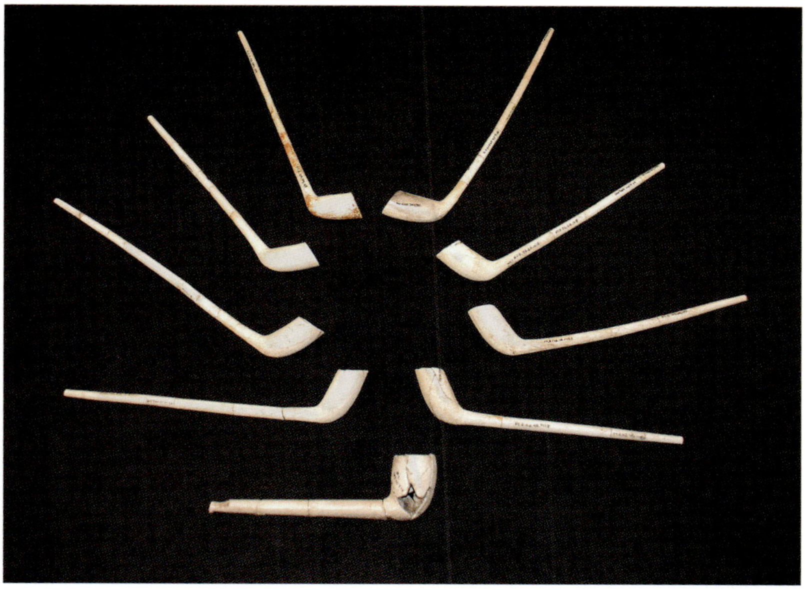

FIG. 9.10. Representative tobacco pipes from the sutling house in Fort Edward. These were among the first pipes to be glued together out of more than four thousand fragments, a very slow and tedious process!

from the 1950s excavation at Fort William Henry are also stored in that museum. (The pipes from one of the boxes appear in fig. 9.7.)

The sutling house in Fort Edward is the only setting where we have pinpointed the storage of pipes that were intended for sale but that had not yet been used. (This is indicated by the lack of tobacco stains inside the bowls.) Altogether, we found 4,298 fragments of stems and bowls, many clustered in a single pile on the cellar floor of the sutling house (fig. 9.8). A majority of the stems had a stem hole diameter of $\frac{4}{64}$ inch, although the holes ranged from $\frac{3}{64}$ to $\frac{6}{64}$ inch in diameter (see appendix). We are systematically gluing these pipe fragments back together for exhibit purposes, although this is a time-consuming task given the size of the collection (figs. 1.5, 9.9, and 9.10). Smoking pipes, and no doubt tobacco itself, were major commodities in the sutling house, perhaps responsible for a significant portion of that business's income.

10

"I Think I May Make Many Reflections on My Own Life & what I Have Seen"
—Jabez Fitch, Jr.
(December 31, 1757)

Conclusions

HAS OUR EXCAVATION into a 1750s' sutling house, most likely the residence and business place of a "Mr. Best," taught us anything new? What do the artifacts from this and other eighteenth-century military camps tell us about the provisioning of the British Army on the frontier of colonial America? Can we say anything about activities or supplies within a tavern frequented by British soldiers or officers? How do our findings compare with those at other British military sites of the period?

Life in the eighteenth century was no doubt difficult for British armies far from home, and survival within the northern reaches of the Colony of New York not only required men who were "Extreem Resolute" (Fitch, Jr. 1968:19), but it necessitated massive provisioning as supplies were moved north from Albany, along the Hudson River, and to frontier outposts where many thousands of men required support from the British Crown. Food, shelter, weapons, tools, and clothing were some of their more obvious needs, and clearly these efforts were generally successful, because these armies, once provisioned, ultimately won the war with France (fig. 10.1).

For many years my colleagues and I excavated tents, huts, and barracks, the "living areas" within the encampments of Fort Edward and Lake George. We found that the remains of structures on Rogers Island chiefly contained fragments of weaponry and ammunition, a few coins, a few knives, quite a few butchered bones from soldiers' meals, and occasional sherds of delft, unrefined stoneware, and wine bottle fragments. Artifacts found within Fort William Henry were similar, reflecting occupancy by the same armies and during the same years. On the other hand, the Lake George Battlefield Park (Fort George) contained some artifacts that were later in time, demonstrating the re-use of that site during the Revolutionary War. In stark contrast, we have now discovered that the material culture contained within a

FIG. 10.1. British reenactors re-fight the 1757 battle at Fort William Henry on September 16, 2007. The French won the original battle, but this time there were no casualties!

civilian sutling house of that period was different. The contents of the sutling house in Fort Edward were often richer—in variety and in value—than artifacts at the campsites we have dug, and the house contained numerous wine glasses, tobacco pipes, knives and forks, coins, delft bowls, white salt-glazed stoneware cups and saucers, and even two pewter plates. This artifact assemblage reinforces our interpretation that this house served as a tavern, but it also means that the sutlers (Mr. Best and his employees, or their successors) lived quite well. They were able to provide quality merchandise—and seemingly a pleasant dining experience—to the soldiers and officers who frequented this establishment. That an officer as senior as Col. James Montresor would dine here occasionally certainly suggests that this was a tavern worth visiting.

Comprehensive coverage of every artifact ever found at the encampments in Fort Edward and Lake George would be a daunting undertaking, and that has not been a goal of this book. Rather, I have tried to present a diverse range of material culture, representing many of the activities engaged in by British armies. I hope that the discovery of each button, coin, delft bowl, and musket ball will help every reader to imagine the coat that lost it, the soldier that dropped it, the officer that ate or drank from it, and the musket that fired it. The artifacts of the armies that shaped America cast a powerful spell over us, even two hundred and fifty years after they were broken or lost. I firmly believe that no archeologist can resist the thrill of uncovering the traces of early military life that lie buried beneath modern towns. New York State was the setting for many of the most significant forts, battlefields, and encampments of both the French and Indian War and the American Revolution, more so than any other colony, and clearly very few communities can equal the historic importance of Fort Edward and Lake George. Artifacts that have survived from the eighteenth century help to tell the story of life on the northern frontier, and, thanks to ongoing archeological projects, there will be many more stories to tell.

It is difficult to compare the contents of our sutling house to other sites precisely because other eighteenth-century sutling houses have not been dug. If instead the artifact comparison is made to Fort Michilimackinac in Michigan, the most thoroughly documented fort of the period (Stone 1974; Evans 2003), then there are a great many differences in what has been found. Michilimackinac has significant numbers of finger rings, crucifixes, tinkling cones, glass trade beads, strike-a-lights, kettles, fishhooks, bale seals, and other artifact types that are poorly represented—if at all—in the military encampments in Fort Edward and Lake George. In the end, though, this should not be surprising because of the longer period of occupation at Michilimackinac, by French and British armies and traders who had more diverse sources of supplies and who traded extensively with Native Americans. By the 1750s, the New York sites thoroughly reflected English material culture, and trade with Native peoples was not a principal function of these encampments.

Artifacts at the New York State camps and forts, while perhaps not revealing evidence for cultural diversity, include sizeable numbers of buttons, buckles, cufflinks, gunflints, musket balls, knives, wine bottles, and tobacco pipes, and these are located just about everywhere. Especially frequent and distinctive at the New York sites are the many woodworking and earth-moving tools: the numerous axes, spades, shovels, and fascine knives. These were the implements required for clearing the forests, digging the moats, and building the earthworks around each fort.

In considering everything that is (and is not) found in collections in Fort Edward and Lake George, it may be that the best artifact comparison of all is to the materials recovered from Fort Ligonier in Pennsylvania. Ligonier was built in 1758, a British timber and earth fort "surrounded by log entrenchments" (Grimm 1970:7) and excavated in the early 1960s. Nearly all of the artifacts excavated in Fort Edward and Lake George are identical to those at Ligonier, except that the Pennsylvania fort had better preservation conditions, resulting in the survival of such things as shoes and leather items.

To an archeologist, artifact analysis is one of the very best ways to learn more about the early armies that occupied and fought in colonial America. Over the past fifty years, the many excavations at military sites in northern New York State have recovered large numbers of period artifacts that permit useful insights into eighteenth-century life. Undeniably, very few additional documents will be discovered from this time period, but the artifacts left behind by British armies will continue to inform and impress us as we study the "Men [who] were Extreem Resolute" (Fitch, Jr. 1968:19) during the British colonial wars. The artifacts we are now discovering are a fascinating part of their legacy to modern generations of Americans.

Appendix

Artifact Totals for the Fort Edward Sutling House, 2001–2008

We have excavated and recovered perhaps eighty percent of the contents of a single merchant's house that burned and collapsed during the French and Indian War. However, we have sampled only a very small proportion of the dumps that surrounded the building, and we have yet to excavate any of the other sutling houses from within the larger sutlers' camp. Our sample size may also have been reduced by salvage efforts made at the time the building burned, and by subsequent years of looting by treasure hunters who no doubt would have removed some of the better artifacts.

All the same, this listing provides a rare look at the artifacts contained within a distinctive class of store and tavern that was critical for the survival of eighteenth-century (and later) armies. Significantly, it provides the first quantitative archeological evidence for the importance of alcohol, tobacco, and personal clothing items within the supplies sold to a British army on the New York frontier.

Weaponry/Ammunition

musket cock with flint	1
musket cock	1
musket ball	105 (all calibers)
lead shot	153 (1 chewed)
lead slag	89
lead sprue	20
gunflint	41
musket side plate with screws (Brown Bess)	1
ramrod pipe	2
brass sling swivel	1
bayonet (and fragments)	5
brass wrist escutcheon	2
brass butt plate (Brown Bess)	1
brass scabbard holder (frog)	1
scabbard tip	2
lead ingot	1 (216.5 g), 1 (223.7 g), 1 (24.5 g), 1 (464.7 g)

Bone & Shell Fragments

mammal and bird bones	4,037
fish bones	53
beaver teeth	11
other mammal teeth	157
tooth with bone	10
freshwater mussel shell fragments	363
eggshell fragments (brown)	28

Glass Fragments

wine bottle (olive-green)	9,113
tableware	1,080
aqua curved (bottle)	298
medicine and vial	208
case bottle	94
green curved (bottle)	21
bottle seal (with greyhounds)	1

Ceramic Sherds

delft	2,936
—complete delft ointment jars	2
white salt-glazed stoneware	840
—with "scratch blue" decoration	149
redware	687
porcelain	269
unrefined stoneware	167
Rhenish stoneware	1
buff-bodied slip-decorated earthenware	1

Cutlery

cutlery handle (knife or fork)	7
fork/fork fragment	15
knife/knife fragment	18
pewter spoon handle	2

Pewter

pewter plate, ten inches diameter	2
pewter fragments	3

Copper Fragments

copper alloy sheeting	26
copper kettle material	95
copper kettle rim	1

Tools and Equipment

ice creeper	2
whetstone	3
horseshoe	2
horseshoe nail	15
ox shoe	12
fragments of wagon wheel hardware	48
felling axe head	1
belt axe head	1
brass fragments	8
brass ferrule	1
chisel, hand wrought	3
file	2
hammerhead	1
padlock	2
key	8
brass book clasp	1
iron pan handle (cookingware)	1
barrel hoop fragments	56
hook with pintle type end	2
punch	2
blade for a spade	1
steelyard (for weighing)	1
stirrup	1
lead seal	1
brass chatelaine with chain	1

Architectural

nails:	
—rose head	8,078
—T-head	127
—L-head	2
screw	9
staples driven into wood	14
window glass fragments	3,512
spike	3
latch bar catch	4
latch plate	1
latch, thumb	1
pintle	8
pintle with hinge	1
sash weight	1
hinge fragments	26
hinge, shutter	1
door lock	4

Personal Adornment/Clothing

buckles (both dress and utility)	70
buttons	112 (+ 1 regimental)
cufflinks (sleeve links)	6 individual + 2 pairs
clothing hooks and eyes	94
clothing pin with blue head	1
bone comb fragments	4

Coins

British half-pence	38
British farthing	4
French liard (1695)	1
Spanish one-real milled or "pillar" silver coin	3 (all minted in Mexico City)
Spanish half-real milled or "pillar" silver coin	5 (all minted in Mexico City)
Spanish one-bit piece of eight	3 (at least 2 minted in Mexico City)
Spanish one-real silver cob	14
Spanish half-real silver cob	1
Spanish four-reales silver cob	1
Oak Tree Shilling (1652)	1

Glass Trade Beads

navy, hexagonal	2 (1 was recovered in 2009)
navy, wound, round	1
red, tubular	1
light gray, round	1
white with 6 red stripes	1 (recovered in 2009)

Musical Instruments

Jew's harp (mouth harp)	4

Tobacco Pipe Fragments

3/64-inch bore diameters	158
4/64-inch bore diameters	1,957
5/64-inch bore diameters	565
6/64-inch bore diameters	13
bowl fragments	1,605

Further Reading

Adler, Winston. 1986. An Island Dig. *Adirondack Life* July/August: 87–88, 91.

Beaudry, Mary C. 2006. *Findings: The Material Culture of Needlework and Sewing*. New Haven, Conn.: Yale University Press.

Brown, Margaret Kimball. 1971. Glass from Fort Michilimackinac: A Classification System for Eighteenth Century Glass. *Michigan Archaeologist* 17(3–4): 97–215.

Calver, William L., and Reginald Bolton. 1950. *History Written with Pick and Shovel*. New York: The New-York Historical Society.

Campbell, J. Duncan. 1958. Investigations at the French Village, Fort Ticonderoga, NY. *Bulletin of the Ft. Ticonderoga Museum* 9(2): 143–155.

Delo, David M. 1998. *Peddlers and Post Traders: The Army Sutler on the Frontier*. Helena, Mont.: Kingfisher Books.

Evans, Lynn L. M. 2003. *Keys to the Past: Archaeological Treasures of Mackinac*. Mackinac Island, Mich.: Mackinac State Historic Parks.

Feister, Lois M. 1984a. Building Materials Indicative of Status Differentiation at the Crown Point Barracks. *Historical Archaeology* 18(1): 103–107.

———. 1984b. Material Culture of the British Soldier at "His Majesty's Fort of Crown Point" on Lake Champlain, New York, 1759–1783. *Journal of Field Archaeology* 11(2): 123–132.

Feister, Lois M., and Paul R. Huey. 1985. Archaeological Testing at Fort Gage, A Provincial Redoubt of 1758 Lake George, New York. *The Bulletin and Journal of Archaeology for New York State* 90: 40–59.

Fitch, Jabez, Jr. 1968. *The Diary of Jabez Fitch, Jr., in the French and Indian War, 1757*, 2nd ed. Fort Edward, N.Y.: Rogers Island Historical Association. Publication No. 1. 3rd ed. in 2007.

Fry, Bruce W. 1984. *"An Appearance of Strength": The Fortifications of Louisbourg*. 2 vols. Studies in Archaeology, Architecture and History. Ottawa: Parks Canada.

Gale, R. R. 2007. *"A Soldier-Like Way": The Material Culture of the British Infantry 1751–1768*. Elk River, Minn.: Track of the Wolf.

Gifford, Stanley M. 1955. *Fort Wm. Henry: A History*. Lake George, N.Y.: Fort William Henry.

Grange, Roger T., Jr. 1987. Excavations at Fort Mackinac, 1980–1982: The Provision Storehouse. *Archaeological Completion Report Series* No. 12. Mackinac Island, Mich.: Mackinac Island State Park Commission.

Grimm, Jacob L. 1970. Archaeological Investigation of Fort Ligonier 1960–1965. *Annals of Carnegie Museum* Vol. 42. Pittsburgh, Pa.

Hamilton, Edward P. 1964. John Henry Lydius, Fur Trader at Fort Edward. *The Bulletin of the Fort Ticonderoga Museum* XI(5): 270–280.

Hamilton, T. M. 1976. Firearms on the Frontier: Guns at Fort Michilimackinac 1715–1781. *Reports in Mackinac History and Archaeology* No. 5. Mackinac Island, Mich.: Mackinac Island State Park Commission.

Hamilton, T. M., and K. O. Emery. 1988. Eighteenth Century Gunflints from Fort Michilimackinac and Other Colonial Sites. *Archaeological Completion Report Series* No. 13. Mackinac Island, Mich.: Mackinac Island State Park Commission.

Hanson, Lee H., and Dick Ping Hsu. 1975. *Casements and Cannonballs. Archeological Investigations at Fort Stanwix, Rome, New York*. Publications in Archeology 14. Washington, D.C.: National Park Service.

Harrington, Jean C. 1957. *New Light on Washington's Fort Necessity*. Richmond, Va.: Eastern National Park and Monument Association.

Heldman, Donald P. 1980. Coins at Michilimackinac. *Historical Archaeology* 14: 82–107.

Henshaw, William. 1909. The Orderly Book of Lt. William Henshaw, May 9, 1759–Nov. 28, 1759. *Transactions and Collections of the American Antiquarian Society* 11:185–254.

Hill, William H. 1929. *Old Fort Edward Before 1800*. Fort Edward, N.Y.: Privately Printed.

———. 1956. *Fort Edward, The End of Nineteenth Century and Later as I Remember*. Fort Edward, N.Y.: Fort Edward Historical Association.

Jones, Olive R., and E. Ann Smith. 1985. *Glass of the British Military, ca. 1755–1820*. Studies in Archaeology, Architecture and History. Ottawa: Parks Canada.

Karklins, Karlis, ed. 2000. *Studies in Material Culture Research*. California, Pa.: The Society for Historical Archaeology.

Kolltviet, Gjermund. 2006. *Jew's Harps in European Archaeology*. British Archaeological Reports International Series, 1500. Oxford, England: Archaeopress.

Liston, Maria A., and Brenda J. Baker. 1995. Reconstructing the Massacre at Fort William Henry, New York. *International Journal of Osteoarchaeology* 6: 28–41.

Majot, Sarah. 1993. Phase I Cultural Resource Investigations for the NMPC Birch Avenue Substation, Glens Falls, Warren County, New York. Albany, N.Y.: Collamer & Associates.

———. 1994. Phase 2 Report of Work in Progress for the Birch Avenue Substation, Lake George, Warren County, New York. Albany, N.Y.: Collamer & Associates.

———. 1995. Stage 2/3 Cultural Resource Investigations for the NMPC Birch Avenue Archaeological Site, Town of Lake George, Warren County, New York. Albany, N.Y.: Collamer & Associates.

Miller, J. Jefferson II, and Lyle M. Stone. 1970. Eighteenth-Century Ceramics from Fort Michilimackinac: A Study in Historical Archaeology. *Smithsonian Studies in History and Technology* No. 4. Washington, D.C.: Smithsonian Institution Press.

Mossman, Philip L. 1993. *Money of the American Colonies and Confederation*. New York: American Numismatic Society.

Neumann, George C., and Frank J. Kravic. 1975. *Collector's Illustrated Encyclopedia of the American Revolution*. Harrisburg, Pa.: Stackpole Books.

Noel Hume, Ivor. 1970. *A Guide to Artifacts of Colonial America*. New York: Alfred A. Knopf.

Plummer, Don. 1999. *Colonial Wrought Iron: The Sorber Collection*. Ocean Pines, Md.: SkipJack Press.

Robbins, Roland Wells, and Evan Jones. 1959. *Hidden America*. New York: Alfred A. Knopf.

Rogers Island Historical Association. 1986. *Exploring Rogers Island*, 2nd ed. Fort Edward, N.Y.: Rogers Island Historical Association.
Rozell, Matthew. 2002. Report on Sutlers' Outworks. Unpublished manuscript.
Scull, G. D., ed. 1882. The Montresor Journals. *Collections of the New-York Historical Society for the Year 1881*. Vol. XIV:1–581.
Sivilich, Daniel M. 1996. Analyzing Musket Balls to Interpret a Revolutionary War Site. *Historical Archaeology* 30(2): 101–109.
Sons of the Revolution in the State of New York. 1991. *"Come all you Gallant Heroes" The World of the Revolutionary Soldier*. New York: Fraunces Tavern Museum.
Starbuck, David R. 1991. A Retrospective on Archaeology at Fort William Henry, 1952–1993; Retelling the Tale of the Last of the Mohicans. *Northeast Historical Archaeology* 20: 8–26.
———. 1993. Anatomy of a Massacre. *Archaeology* 46: 42–46.
———. 1998. The Big Dig: Looking for Traces of Fort William Henry's Brutal Past. *Adirondack Life* 29: 44–49, 77–78.
———. 1995. (editor) *Archeology in Fort Edward*. Queensbury, N.Y.: Adirondack Community College.
———. 1997a. America's Forgotten War. *Archaeology* 50: 60–63.
———. 1997b. Military Hospitals on the Frontier of Colonial America. *Expedition* 39(1): 33–45.
———. 1999a. Early Military Sites Archaeology in New York State: An Interview with Richard J. Koke. *Northeast Historical Archaeology* 28: 71–88.
———. 1999b. *The Great Warpath*. Hanover, N.H.: University Press of New England.
———. 2001. Beneath the Bubblegum. *Archaeology* 54(1): 22–23.
———. 2002a. Hallowed Ground: Exploring Lake George Battlefield Park. *Adirondack Life: 2002 Annual Guide to the Great Outdoors* XXXIII(4): 14–16, 18–20, 22.
———. 2002b. *Massacre at Fort William Henry*. Hanover, N.H.: University Press of New England.
———. 2004. *Rangers and Redcoats on the Hudson*. Hanover, N.H.: University Press of New England.
———. 2007. Commerce of War. *Archaeology* 60(4): 41–43.
———. 2008a. Colonial America at War! "Sutlers" Provided Fort Edward Soldiers with Much-Needed Relief. *The Journal of the Washington County Historical Society*, pp. 4—11.
———. 2008b. The "Massacre" at Fort William Henry: History, Archaeology, and Re-enactment. *Expedition* 50(1):17–25.
Steele, Ian K. 1990. *Betrayals: Fort William Henry and the "Massacre."* New York: Oxford University Press.
Stone, Lyle. 1974. Fort Michilimackinac, 1715–1781: An Archaeological Perspective on the Revolutionary Frontier. *Anthropological Series*, Vol. 2. Michigan State University, East Lansing, in cooperation with Mackinac Island State Park Commission, Mackinac Island, Mich.
Sullivan, Catherine. 1986. *Legacy of the Machault: A Collection of 18th-Century Artifacts*. Studies in Archaeology, Architecture and History. Ottawa: Parks Canada.
Troiani, Don. 1998. *Don Troiani's Soldiers in America 1754–1865*. Mechanicsburg, Pa.: Stackpole Books.
———. 2001. *Military Buttons of the American Revolution*. Gettysburg, Pa.: Thomas Publications.

Vandrei, Charles E. 2001. The Lake George Battlefield Park: Looking to the Future through the Past. *Conservationist* 55(4): 26–28.

Wickman, Donald H. (Transcriber and Editor). 1997. "Breakfast on Chocolate": The Diary of Moses Greenleaf, 1777. *The Bulletin of the Fort Ticonderoga Museum* XV(6): 482–506.

Yeoman, R. S. 2009. *The Official Red Book: A Guide Book of United States Coins 2010*. Atlanta, Ga.: Whitman Publishing.

Zaboly, Gary Stephen. 2004. *A True Ranger: The Life and Many Wars of Major Robert Rogers*. Garden City Park, N.Y.: Royal Blockhouse.